To Avril
With lots of
love from Philip.
April 13rd 1982

Mosaics in Needlepoint

Also by Xenia Parker

WORKING WITH LEATHER
DESIGNING FOR CRAFTS

Mosaics in Needlepoint

FROM STONE TO STITCHERY
Xenia Ley Parker

Charles Scribner's Sons   New York

All art, unless otherwise indicated, is by Xenia L. Parker

Copyright © 1977 Xenia Ley Parker

Library of Congress Cataloging in Publication Data

Parker, Xenia Ley.
    Mosaics in needlepoint.

    Bibliography: p. 139
    Includes index.
    1. Canvas embroidery—Patterns. 2. Mosaics. I. Title.
TT778.C3P38   746.4′4   77-5045
ISBN 0-684-15035-2
ISBN 0-684-15036-0 pbk.

1 3 5 7 9 11 13 15 17 19 Q/C 20 18 16 14 12 10 8 6 4 2
1 3 5 7 9 11 13 15 17 19 Q/P 20 18 16 14 12 10 8 6 4 2

Printed in the United States of America.

Contents

Introduction

THE ONGOING CHALLENGE to needle-pointers everywhere is the pleasurable and rewarding search for exciting designs and patterns that are exceptionally well suited to the requirements of their art. One of the most fascinating veins of design ideas is mosaics. Largely untapped as a source of inspiration for needlework, mosaics dating from ancient times right up to the present offer myriad possibilities.

In mosaics small individual units are joined together on a background medium to form an overall design in the completed work. These patterns are logically comparable to, and can be transposed to meet the structural framework of, needlepoint canvas design. Each mosaic chip is as essential to the whole as is each stitch and color in needlepoint. The angularity of motifs created by mosaic techniques is intrinsically helpful in planning attractive needlepoint.

Once you see how well these forms work together, you'll be impatient to get started on your own mosaic in needlepoint. For those who want a refresher, basic needlepoint techniques and stitches, as well as those best suited to this design style, are detailed. Then the transition from mosaic to finished needlepoint is clearly seen as a step-by-step process which you can follow, opening up a new world of design ideas to discover, explore, experiment with, and enjoy.

Mosaics in Needlepoint

CHAPTER ONE

From Stone
to Stitchery

THE QUALITIES of a mosaic are demanding, in terms of just how a subject can be presented. Equally demanding is the structural design of a needlepoint canvas. Surprisingly, you'll find that these unrelated art forms have many things in common, and from this you will understand why mosaics are a uniquely suitable source of design inspiration for your needlepoint stitcheries.

The most traditional form of mosaic is comprised of small square chips of stone or glass known as tesserae. These squares must be worked together to create a design. Each small square fits into the overall work so that you see it as a whole from just a short distance. And so it is with needlepoint canvas, which is woven in a balanced open weave. As the threads of the canvas cross, leaving open spaces that you fill with yarn as you stitch the design, the basic design is also structured on the basis of small squares. If you've ever worked with needlepoint, you know that it is impossible to stitch a true circle. Instead, you stitch a series of small steps to make what appears to be a circle when it is finished. In mosaics the same type of stepped curve is used, with similar results.

When you look at a needlepoint design plan, you most often see it presented in graph form on squared paper, each square representing one stitch on the canvas. To follow the pattern, you make one stitch to correspond to each filled-in square on the graph. As you look at a mosaic done in the squared-chip form, you can discern the separate pieces and could actually follow them in the same manner to create a needlepoint design directly from the mosaic itself. This method is particularly effective when you use a large or gros point canvas and the heavyweight yarn that is suited to it.

Another similarity that exists between needlepoint and mosaics is the fact that both are two-dimensional. Naturally, you can create three-dimensional effects, but both works are done on a flat surface. This relationship can aid you greatly in adapting designs, as there is no need to translate from three dimensions to two, as you would have to do when using an actual object or even a photograph which presents three-dimensional subjects in two-dimensional form. Works created specifically within a two-dimensional framework engender a certain feeling that is shared by mosaics and fine needlepoint designs.

Although the colors that you choose are part of your personal statement, here again a definite relationship can be found. When you work in both needlepoint and mosaics, the colors can be used only within the guidelines of their structural forms. Just as each piece in a mosaic can be one color, each stitch can be one color. Therefore, you work in blocks of color to create the design. For special effects you can blend colors in a method known to artists as "broken colors." These are colors created by small amounts of two or more colors worked with each other in close conjunction so that your eye blends them together when they are seen from a distance. For example, single stitches of yellow and red stitched in one area would appear to be orange when seen from farther away. This technique is found in mosaics and is well known in the works of the Impressionist painters known as Pointillists. The use of broken colors seems to lend a shimmer to the final color that is sometimes more interesting than the actual color would be.

To create the appearance of shading, for depth or realism in a design, use several shades of the color, placing them next to each other in sequence from lightest to darkest. This is done in mosaics and needlepoint as each unit of the design can be only one of the shades. This differs from other art forms, such as painting, in which you can use the same color and merely add black or white to it to create a shaded effect.

For ideas on the actual colors to use, you will

Rabbit with mushrooms and lizard. Roman, first century B.C., mosaic of glass cubes.

Metropolitan Museum of Art, Gift of J. Pierpont Morgan, 1917.

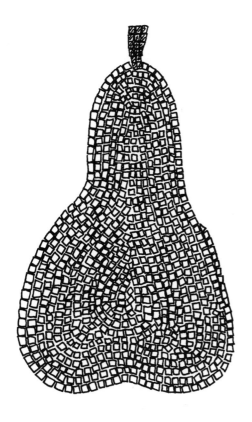

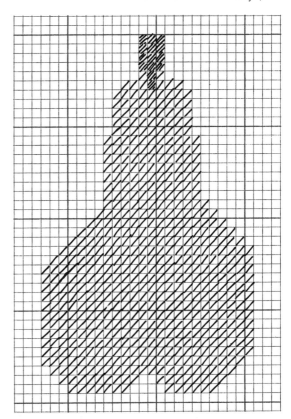

Sketch of a pear as worked in mosaic tesserae.

A needlepoint graph of the same pear.

find that there are mosaics in many styles from which you can draw your own schemes. From the subtle tones used by the ancient Greeks to the brilliance of the colors found in Byzantine works, you'll find a wealth of inspiration.

As you begin to look at mosaics in a new light, you'll see clearly how many of their attributes are related to the kind of design and pattern that work well in needlepoint.

CHAPTER TWO

Mosaic Patterns and Sources

MOSAICS ARE among the oldest surviving art works, because of the durability of the materials employed. When you use the term in its widest sense, including any type of work where many small units are combined to form an overall pattern, mosaics are known that date back to the earliest civilizations in Mesopotamia, five thousand years before the birth of Christ. These works were done to decorate floors and walls with simple repeating geometric patterns. These basic designs were developed in style and technique through the ages, and mosaics are still in wide use today, ranging in scope from unassuming tiled floors to commanding outdoor murals.

The mosaic style with which we are most familiar is made up of small square or sometimes rectangular pieces called tesserae set into a cement base. The tesserae can be made of glass, ceramic, marble, or slate. For different effects stones, pebbles, irregularly shaped chips of marble, and many other small objects can be used. Even kitchen staples such as dried beans can form interesting works. The mosaic covers the entire surface of the work, usually upon a foundation of wood or metal created especially to hold it. Mosaics made in this way are true mosaics.

Inlaid works, called intarsia, quite popular in the Italian Renaissance, are set into a visible background. In these works only the design sections are cut to fit into the background material which remains part of the finished pattern. This is also known as marquetry, particularly used in wood on wood, and *opus sectile* as it was employed in earlier times in marble. The true mosaics are called *opus vermiculatum,* including the figurative works made with square tesserae. The term *opus tesselatum* refers to larger-scale works made with squares, usually in floors or pavements.

Another type of work that fits into the broad classification of mosaics is called Cosmati, after the Italian family that made wide use of it. In Cosmati, floors and most often columns of marble are set with bands of tesserae. A channel is cut into the marble and then a mosaic design or pattern is set into the channel, leaving the unworked areas as part of the design. This style was mainly in use from the seventh to the late thirteenth century.

Comesso is another style that was popular in Italy during the Renaissance. In this type of work, parts of a design were cut to fit flush with each other, covering the background setting completely. Many colors of marble and semiprecious stones were used with fine workmanship to cover tables, floors, and even walls. Many of these works were commissioned by the Medicis and can be seen in Florence today.

Ducks and ducklings. Roman, first century B.C. to first century A.D., marble mosaic.

Metropolitan Museum of Art, Gift of Mrs. W. Bayard Cutting, 1932.

When you look at mosaics hoping to find inspiration for ideas that will work well in needlepoint, all of the various kinds of work can be helpful to you. Each has its own particular style and the results are often quite different in appearance. In general, the pictorial mosaics will probably be the most exciting, as they include animals, birds, fish, flowers, and all manner of living things, as well as representations of people.

Representational mosaics are found throughout recorded history, and the works done by people in different areas and times are still strikingly attractive today. The Aegean Minoans used rounded pebbles for floors and pavements. They also began to use regularly shaped

Cosmati patterns.

Cosmati patterns.

Grotesque. Roman, first century A.D., mosaic of glass cubes.

Metropolitan Museum of Art, Gift of Henry G. Marquand, 1881.

Personification of Spring. Roman, second century A.D., second half, from Antioch, Roman villa at Daphne, mosaic pavement, central panel, 7'5" × h. 8'3".

Metropolitan Museum of Art, Purchase, from Joseph Pulitzer Bequest, 1938.

tesserae in finer pieces that doubtless had an influence on the later Greek mosaics, which were more like their vase paintings than the geometric mosaics of the Minoans.

Perhaps the most widely known mosaics of ancient times are those of the Romans. They perfected the art, using stone and marble tesserae to create floor and wall coverings in houses and outdoor pavements. Most of the existing mosaics from this period are floor or pavement coverings, so it is believed that these were more widespread than the wall designs. Works from the Roman Empire have been found in ancient villas from North Africa to

Peacock in color on white ground. North African, second to fourth century, early Christian, glazed earthenware mosaic wall tile.

Metropolitan Museum of Art, Gift of Kirkor Minassian, 1926.

England. The Roman mosaics are often square or rectangular in shape and have a geometric border enclosing a figurative design with animals and figures of people or gods painstakingly represented. Smaller tesserae are used to form the interior figures in great detail. Several geometric borders are incorporated in some works, giving you many from which to choose your favorites. During the same period a stylized form was also used in three or four colors with less emphasis on realism. These simple designs are created without the meticulous detail in the central figures, using tesserae of the same size and shape throughout the work with little attention to perspective. However, the results are extremely effective and show you how much can be accomplished with a minimum of color.

As the Roman Empire deteriorated and the center of power shifted to Byzantium, the mosaicists' art went with it. By the time Christianity became the official religion and the city of Constantinople was established as the capital of the empire in the fourth century, mosaics had become a chief architectural detail of the walls and ceilings of the newly created Byzantine churches. This is perhaps the best-remembered feature of Byzantine art, as brightly colored glass tesserae were employed to depict awe-inspiring scenes that were larger than life.

Golden backgrounds with figures in many hues were worked as mosaics flourished from the fourth to the eighth centuries. In Ravenna, Italy, many fine mosaics still exist in their original

Passage of the Red Sea. Fifth-century mosaic, reproduction of original in S. Maria Maggiori, Rome.

Metropolitan Museum of Art, Johnston Fund, 1924.

The Archangel Gabriel. Byzantine, reproduction of mosaic from the Church of Hagia Sophia, main apse, Istanbul, 3′ × 4′. Metropolitan Museum of Art, Harris Brisbane Dick Fund, 1943.

glory, with colors that have not paled with time.

In other parts of Italy and Greece mosaics came into wide use in the twelfth century and continued to be popular through the sixteenth century and the flowering of the Italian Renaissance.

As fresco painting grew in popularity and the many technological changes of the Renaissance took place, mosaics began to take a lesser position in the decoration of newly built cathedrals. Domenico Ghirlandaio, a painter of the fifteenth century, called them a sort of eternal painting. As such, their own particular style was gone and mosaics, like the Byzantine Empire which nurtured them, lost their power and strength.

Mosaics continued to be produced intermittently but it was not until the twentieth century that the art was truly revived. In both Europe and the Americas mosaics rebounded as artists and craftspeople began to rediscover the art form. Today, mosaics are created in many materials for many purposes ranging from entire

Panel showing the Empress Theodora and members of her court. Byzantine, 536–547 A.D., reproduction of the original mosaic in the Church of San Vitale, Ravenna.
Metropolitan Museum of Art, Fletcher Fund, 1925.

outdoor walls on museums, universities, and other public buildings to small sculptural works.

As you seek out mosaics you'll find that there is a wealth of pictorial information in books on the subject, many of which can be found in your local library. The churches of Ravenna often are detailed in oversize formats that will be well worth your while to look up. There is a list of recommended sources at the end of this book for volumes that depict mosaics in both color and black and white from many periods in history and many areas of the world.

Museums are another place where you can see mosaics; being able to study the actual work will enhance your understanding. Larger art museums, such as the Metropolitan Museum of Art in New York City, have entire sections of ancient pavements in their collections that are both beautiful and fascinating. The work of modern artists can also be seen in museums such as the Museum of Contemporary Crafts in New York City, and in galleries when special exhibits are held.

In many cities mosaics are a part of a building's design, both inside and out. In older buildings simple geometrics and other basic patterns are found in tiled floors in entryways and halls. These are a good source for borders or small units in a design. They have been placed in newer public buildings as murals and even outside walls and, of course, are part of many houses of worship. In short, you will find mosaics all around you once you start to look for them.

CHAPTER THREE

How to
Adapt Designs

WHEN YOU FIND a mosaic design that appeals to you, there are several ways to transfer your idea from inspiration to canvas. The method you choose depends to a great extent upon how you plan to use the design in a mosaic.

Adapting the design as a whole is possible for many mosaics with simple forms. If you want to adapt a simple design, you can copy the outlines of the mosaic as is, using lightweight artist's paper called vellum, which is translucent, or tracing paper. Another very effective method is

Line drawing of the Roman mosaic, page 2.

Repeating pattern of birds and medallions, from a ceiling mosaic in Ravenna.

Leafy scroll within another shape, detail from the grotesque design, page 8.

Cupid rowing, a detail from a larger sea mosaic which becomes an entire scene in itself.

Cave canem, a white and black mosaic with small touches of red from Pompeii.

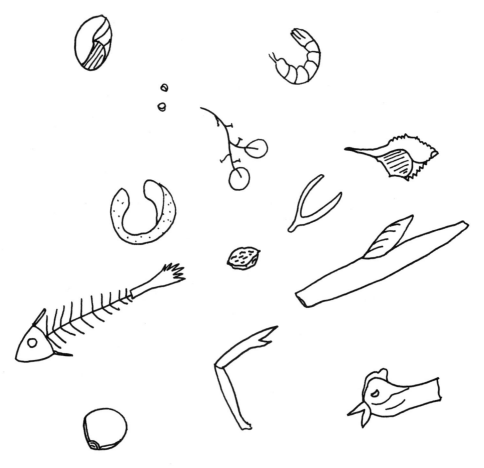

Asaroton, a Roman unswept floor design mosaic, the leftovers from a feast.

Dionysius on the Panther, Delos, second century B.C.

Detail, Dionysius.

Detail, panther.

Greco-Roman mosaic detail.

to use a photostat. Luckily, many libraries have copying machines and you can often make a photostatic copy right on the spot. These copies do lose a lot of detail so it is a good idea to draw in any parts that are not clear while you have the original on hand. If you are working with a color photograph of a mosaic, the photostat or your drawing will be in black and white. When you want to use the same shades in your work, indicate them on the copy using letters or symbols if the areas are too small to write the full names of the colors within their boundaries. When you want to choose your own color scheme this step is unnecessary.

If you are an experienced needlepointer you may want to copy an entire mosaic that is quite complex. In this case you will need to make a detailed version of the original design so that none of the details are omitted. If you can copy the design without trouble you can base your needlepoint canvas on that drawing. However, many of the works will be hard to do in this manner, and the type of copying machine found in most libraries won't give you enough clarity of detail. In this instance you should have a professional photostat made for you by a pho-

tographic store. All of the details will show well, as long as the photograph from which you are working is clear. Most photostats are negative, with white lines on black paper, but you can ask for a positive version as well, which will be much easier to use. Another possibility is to get a reproduction from an art museum. They come in many sizes and are usually in color. Postcards are also helpful in that you can enlarge the designs, as described in the next chapter.

Seeking out parts of a complex mosaic and enlarging them for use as whole designs or combining them with other motifs can provide you with hundreds of ideas. You'll find that large mosaics include many details that are lovely by themselves. The examples shown here were all drawn from minute parts of wall- or ceiling-size works. You can find these details just by looking for them, even in works that don't appeal to you as a whole. When you see a large mosaic, study it carefully and analyze all the parts that go into the total design. If you see even a single flower that you like, copy it. You may find that when you have compiled many separate design motifs they will start to come together in your mind's eye to form a design. Keeping a notebook with motifs for figures and borders that you have seen in many works will be quite useful to you in formulating your own designs. Whenever something catches your eye, you can put it into your design collection. Even if you can't think of an immediate project that the motif is suited to as you include it, at some future date you may find that it's just the idea you need.

As you use small design ideas, you can add definition to them if they seem too flat when they are enlarged. To get the detail that may be lacking when you make a small motif larger, you should look at other sources that depict that idea. As an example, if you have enlarged a small animal form, look at actual photographs of that animal for the correct coloration. Paintings and other renderings of the same type of shape or figure will also give you an idea of where and how to add detail to an object.

From the Palace of Khirbat al-Mafjar, a floor mosaic in the baths, Jerusalem, eighth century A.D.

Detail from a vault mosaic, fourth century A.D., S. Costanza, Rome.

Detail from a floor mosaic in Aquileia, fourth century A.D.

Ducks and ducklings, drawing of the Roman mosaic, page 5.

Mesopotamian columns, mosaic design formed with
inset cone-shaped tesserae in black and white.

Phoenix, from Antioch, sixth century A.D.

Detail of Moorish pattern, from Morocco.

Birds entering the Ark. Section of Ark panel, San Marco, Venice.

Repeating pavement design, Moorish, from Alhambra.

Backgrounds in figurative mosaics are, for the most part, solid colors. This is done to set off the figures to their best advantage and it works quite well in needlepoint designs. You'll find that a central design with a solid-color background and an outline or simple border is a very effective plan to follow for many works. As an added bonus you can often key the background color to the intended use of the object, such as the color scheme in a room in which it will be placed, with little change in the hues of the central figure. When you are using basic shapes you can enliven a one-color background by using a patterned or textural stitch instead of the basic needlepoint tent stitch.

Rabbit running, detail from Roman mosaic.

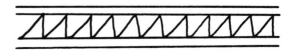

Border designs from many sources; four patterns with triangular shapes.

In other works the background itself is the dominant theme. In an all-over geometric or abstract mosaic-style needlepoint the entire area is stitched with a repeating pattern or series of shapes that are complete in themselves and cover the whole canvas. An excellent source for patterns that are suited to this type of design is Moroccan tile work, which includes complex geometrics that beautifully carpet the walls and floors of many buildings. These mosaics are somewhat like the Oriental rug designs in flavor, and you'll find their endless variety fascinating.

Borders are found in abundance in mosaics, particularly those of antiquity. You'll discover so many patterns that you will probably want to use them in needlepoint of all sorts, even on works that are otherwise unrelated to mosaics. The examples of border patterns shown here will give you an idea of the infinite range of border designs from which you can choose.

When planning a border for a project you should take the dimensions of the stitched area into consideration. When you are creating the border you should always remember that you don't want it to overpower the central features so that you see more border than anything else. You are aiming for a balance between the parts

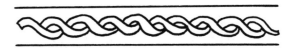

Wave-shaped border designs.

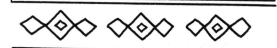

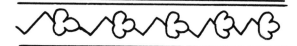

Borders with linked diamond forms.

Borders with squared shapes.

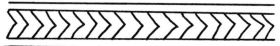

Zigzag borders.

of the work so that the border is what it is meant to be: an attractive outline that frames your design. In some cases no border at all is needed. The best way to judge this is to make a paper model of your entire design. After you have drawn in all its parts, choose a border that you think is suited to the design and draw the pattern for it on a separate strip of paper. Then place the border strip along one end of the design and see how it looks. If you like it, draw

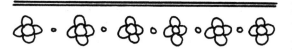

Abstract floral borders.

it in on the design itself, surrounding the central area as it will be in the actual stitchery. Then you'll be able to decide on the total impact of the design. As your work is your own statement, you should be the one to decide just what will go into it. If you find that the border is not suitable, you can make other paper strips with different borders and try them out without drawing the border onto the design itself and later having to change it. You can save the border strips you have drawn for other designs if they don't seem just right for the one on which you are working. They will always come in handy.

When you have tried out several borders and none looks correct, perhaps the design is the type that doesn't need a patterned outline. In this case you have several options. The first is to omit the border altogether. The second is to try a series of outlines in the colors that are found in the design. You can use two or more, making each outline one stitch wide, which often sets off a design quite well. Another idea is to vary the width of each outline so that your border actually consists of stripes of color in different widths. You can also make a border out of a band of one color, possibly using a different stitch for interest. As you can see, there is no limit to the number of variations possible.

Mosaics provide other kinds of design inspiration for needlepoint. When you adapt the design itself you can use the design as your main objective and stitch the work in the basic tent stitch. This creates the design with changes of color, as all of the stitches are the same. As a variation on this theme, you can choose to work areas of the design in different stitches to add texture.

Another design idea is to create a mosaic in stitches by working with square or rectangular stitch units, as described in chapter six. These stitches can be worked in the same manner as a mosaic so that you can create a design by working one stitch unit for each tile in the mosaic itself. You can also use this technique to create a mosaic effect on a design that you have created without reference to mosaics or one found in another source. Working with these stitches is challenging when applied to any design and they will give your work a unique quality, even when you are executing a simple design.

Using a large-mesh canvas with fine wool rug yarns that are sized to suit the larger openings will give you a true mosaic effect as you stitch in the larger gros point stitches. These works are a pleasure to do; you see the results all the sooner and they are easy to stitch. In this type of work you'll find that you can create wall-size hangings, much like mosaic murals in scope and design. Any room is enhanced by the warmth and beauty of a needlepoint mural created especially for that room, adding a personal touch that few paintings or other works that you would buy ever can.

And so it is with needlepoint objects of all kinds that you create from first sketch to last stitch. You'll discover a double enjoyment, in the planning and stitching, and then in the finished works themselves.

CHAPTER FOUR

Setting Up a Design on Needlepoint Canvas

PLANNING THE SHAPE and size of a project, using its dimensions to make a paper pattern, setting up the design to suit the canvas, transferring the design to the canvas, and using a chart for the actual stitching are all essential parts of how well your design will work. Even if you've never done an original work before, you'll find that you have no difficulties when you follow the steps for preparation of a canvas in the correct order.

Planning a project isn't hard, once you decide what it is you want to make. Many articles can be made in needlepoint using paper patterns that you can make yourself. As a basic example, if you want to make a pillow, you can buy a pillow form of known dimensions and cut out a piece of heavy paper in that size to create the amount of space that you will fill with an appropriate design. If you have a pillow on hand that you would like to cover, measure its width and length. Then mark these measurements on a large sheet of paper for your basic pattern. When you are planning a wall hanging, make a paper pattern of the size that you think will best suit the wall and the room in which the wall is found. To test it out, tape the paper pattern, cut to shape, to the wall itself. If it seems too large, too small, too wide, or too long, you can alter the pattern easily by cutting it down or adding new strips of paper to make it

larger. This type of experimentation is quite helpful as you will know before you begin to plan the design just what size it will be and how much space you have to work with to create the design.

For more complex articles that require seams or other means of assemblage, you can make a pattern by carefully measuring and marking on paper all the dimensions of a similar article that you have on hand. Using an existing object in this way, you can form a plan for a new article with the same function that you will create yourself. Sometimes you can even use the article itself, as when you cover a book or make a seat cover for a chair that you already own. When planning a paper version of an object that you want to make, you should try it out by taping the parts together after you have marked and cut them out on heavy paper. When the paper model works, carefully cut it apart. If there are any seams, allow for them by adding $\frac{1}{2}$ inch to each side where a seam occurs. Also remember to add at least $\frac{1}{2}$ inch to all sides of any stitched work, as the stitching itself pulls the canvas in a bit as you stitch. This happens in all needlepoint, so you should allow for it before you begin. When you are planning something large, you should add up to 1 inch, just to be sure that when you have finished stitching you will have enough needlepointed area to

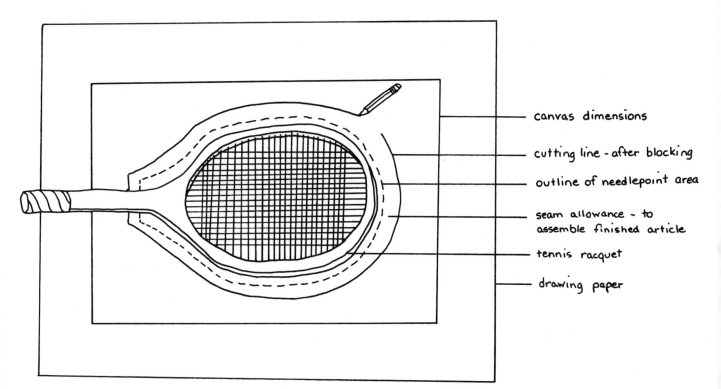

canvas dimensions

cutting line - after blocking

outline of needlepoint area

seam allowance - to assemble finished article

tennis racquet

drawing paper

Making a pattern using an existing object as a guide.

complete your project without any blank canvas showing at the sides or on any seams.

Another allowance you make on paper patterns is for any folds that occur. For example, if you are making a book cover, you can trace the outlines needed for your project by opening the book and placing it face down on a piece of heavy paper. Trace around it for the basic shape and size. Then close the book and fold the paper around it. As you do this, you'll see that when the book is closed you actually need a larger shape to cover it adequately. In general, this type of fold allowance should be about ½ inch. Even if you add too much in the way of allowances to an article, you'll be in a much better position when you're finished than if you had added too little. Unless you've left a wide canvas border around the stitched area, there's not much you can do if your stitchery turns out too small. On the other hand, if it's too large, you can just make the seam or any other finishing device a bit wider, your needlepoint will

Placing a design so that it faces in the right direction in the finished article. The dotted lines show where the folds occur in the article as it is assembled. Note how the design focus changes to suit the object.

Book cover.

look perfect, and the few rows of extra stitches that you did will have been well worth your while.

To plan original patterns without using an actual object as a pattern, use a paper version to figure out how many parts there are, how large they must be, and so on. Working with a paper version to try out all kinds of variations is fun and quite easy, and you can make several models of your project before you decide on the one that's just right.

When it comes to hard things to figure out, such as frame pocketbooks or complete reupholstery of a chair, you'll need the advice of an expert who will assemble the article once you have finished the stitching. In this case you can find out beforehand how much the piece will cost to be mounted and then, if you want to proceed, the person who will finish the mounting will provide the pattern. Slippers with leather bottoms and binding are also made in this way—the professional who makes them gives you the pattern to follow in the correct size before you begin to stitch. Wall hangings and pillows may also be professionally mounted, but these are things that you can successfully complete on your own.

Setting up the design to suit the basic outlines of your pattern is done once you are completely satisfied with the pattern itself. This helps you in the placement of the design, and you can see just where it will be when the article is finished. There are a few basics you should keep in mind to aid you in the correct placement of the major parts of the design. These guidelines allow you to put the parts together so that the design faces in the right direction.

For book covers and other objects that fold along the left-hand edge, look at the basic pattern, mark the fold lines, and place the design on the right-hand side of the pattern so that it will be on the front of the cover. When you make things with a fold at the bottom, such as eyeglass cases, mark the fold line and place the design above it. In this case, as you look at the pattern, it will usually be rectangular, with the fold across the middle from one long

Eyeglass case.

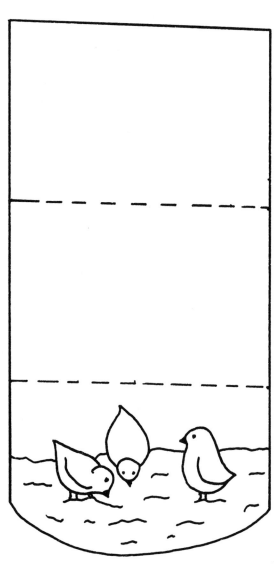

Purse with a flap.

Pillow.

side to the other. Remember to place the design so that it will be right side up when the article is stitched. This may sound elementary but sometimes mistakes of this nature do occur. If you are planning an object with a flap, such as a purse, mark the design at the bottom of the pattern below the fold line for the flap so that when the flap is folded over in the finished article, the design will show correctly. In planning pillows, wall hangings, and other articles that are flat, or are made in separate sections, place the design so that it is well centered in the area. This type of placement is the easiest, as you are working with the area of the pattern in much the same position as it will be in the finished work.

To make the placement of the design easier, use tracing or other lightweight paper. First, trace the outlines of the article itself. On a separate piece of paper trace the design. Then place the outlines over the design. Look through the paper, check the design, and move the outlines until it seems just right. When it does, trace it onto the paper with the outlines on it and you will have the complete design and pattern on one sheet. As you work, you can trace different parts of the design on small sheets of paper and move them around in the same way until you're happy with the layout. Then trace the entire design and outlines onto a single sheet of paper. If you're using a border, work it into the total design pattern in the same manner.

Wall hanging.

Enlarging a design is easy when you find that your design is too small for the project, or when you have adapted it from a small-size source. You'll need several sheets of paper, a ruler, and a pencil. If you don't want to draw on the original design, trace it onto a sheet of paper. Then mark off evenly spaced lines and draw them horizontally across the design. Using the same distance between the lines, do the same thing vertically. One inch is usually a good width to work with. If your design is irregular, it may be easier to outline it with a square or rectangle, whichever it fits into best, for enlargement purposes only. Use the sides of the square or rectangle to measure off and mark the lines on your design. Then take a larger sheet of paper and mark a square or rectangle the size that you want the enlargement to be. Draw the same number of lines in each direction, making sure that they are equally spaced. It doesn't matter how large you make the new set of boxes that are formed by the crossing lines as long as there are as many as are found on the smaller version of the design. Then, working box by box, redraw the design on the larger sheet of paper. Even if you can't draw, for some reason when you break up a design into parts and draw each one within a limited area it is not hard to do. This method works with any type of enlargement, even when you are enlarging into a shape of different proportions. As long as you make the same number of boxes on each version as you redraw the original design, its own lines stretch out to fit the new form. To make your final enlargement clearer, trace it again, leaving out the crossing lines of the grid you drew.

To change the size or proportions severely, you may find it easier to work in two steps: for example, make the first set of lines on the original 1 inch apart and the second grid with the lines 2 inches apart; the final version could have lines 4 inches apart. When you are changing the proportions, only the grid on the original will consist of squares. On the subsequent set of boxes that you make, because the proportions

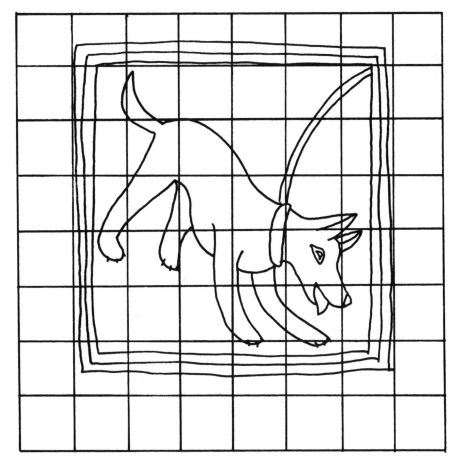

Enlarging a design with a grid, original version.

have been changed, the grid will be made up of a series of rectangles instead of squares. This is correct, but do check that there are the same number in each version. As you make the lines, you may find that the larger version does not divide evenly. If this happens, place the ruler on one corner of the design enlargement's outline. Hold it so that it goes across to the opposite corner and slowly move it up along one edge until an even measurement occurs. As you move the ruler, it will form an angle to the side you're working on. Then mark off each line that you need, using the inch measurements on the ruler. As you have moved the ruler up on an angle, the distance between each line as you

draw it will not be the same as the reading on the ruler, but the lines will be the same distance apart throughout. Do the same to the other side if necessary.

To make a design smaller, do the same thing in reverse by marking a grid on the large version and then drawing an outline and a grid with smaller distances between the lines for the smaller version. Then proceed as in enlarging, drawing one part of the design at a time within the boundaries of one box on the grid.

To enlarge or make a design smaller when you want to use the same proportions, you can have a photostat made. When you take the design to have it copied, tell the person what

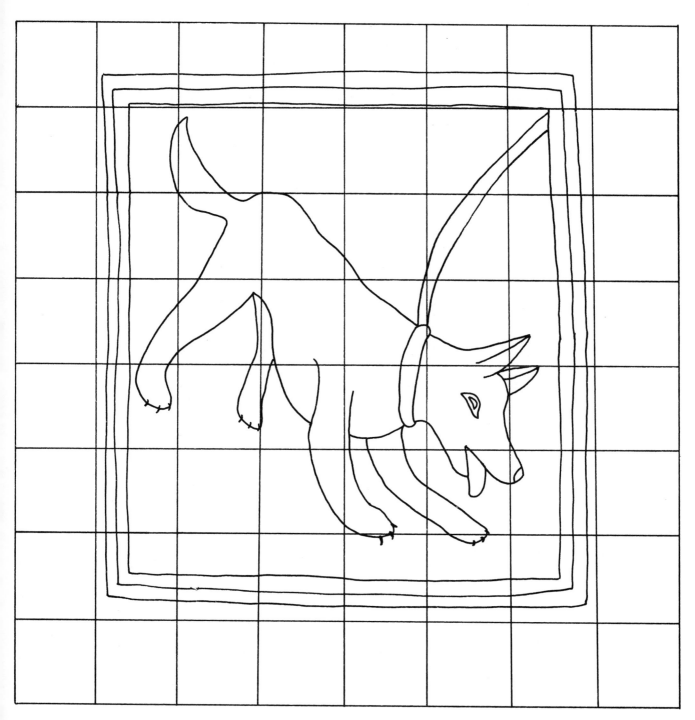

Enlarged design.

TOP

Enlarged design in different proportions. Note that the number of boxes in the grid remains the same, while their shape is elongated to alter the original proportions.

size you want the new version to be. Make sure that you get the positive (white paper with black lines) photostat; it is much easier to use. This method won't work if you want to change the proportions, as you can only have a photostat made larger or smaller in the same shape as the original.

Color schemes can be chosen at any time as you plan a project, but an ideal time is when you have the complete paper pattern with the design drawn on it. If you have a good idea of what you want, color it in with water paints, felt-tip pens, or even crayons. You can use anything that will let you see how the color scheme looks on the design. If you are undecided, trace the entire pattern several times, or get several photostats and color in each version with a different color scheme.

Should you want to consider various color schemes, there are many sources for inspiration. The first one to check is the intended use of the article. If you are planning to use it in a specific room, go into that room and look around at the colors that are already there. Think of a scheme that will harmonize with its surroundings, perhaps using the same basic colors with small areas of new, brighter colors for accents. If you are making something as a gift for someone, think of his or her color preferences, not yours. You can tell which ones your friends or relatives prefer just by looking at the clothes they wear or the colors in their house or apartment. If you're making something for yourself, do entirely as you please.

For further color ideas, see if you can find a color photograph of a mosaic that may have inspired your design, or one from a similar period in history. Look in magazines and fine department or home-furnishing stores to see color schemes that seem effective to you. When it comes to using colors, you'll discover that just about anything goes, as long as you like it and it looks right to you. As with so many things, the old rules are being broken and you no longer have to use a certain color with another because everyone else agrees that you can. Be inde-

pendent and you'll be sure to come out on top.

Transferring the design to the canvas is done when you are sure that your design is complete in every detail. If you plan to work from a chart, draw only the basic outlines of the project itself, following the same procedure. You'll need a ruler, a clear copy of your design, the canvas you are planning to use, and some waterproof, narrow-tip felt marking pens. Before you begin, make sure that the pens are completely waterproof by snipping off a small piece of canvas, drawing a line on it, and wetting the canvas when the line has dried. If the ink runs even the slightest bit, don't use the pen, as you must dampen a finished canvas to block it and the ink will ruin it. There are felt-tip pens made especially for this purpose, but you should check them anyway to be on the safe side. It's also a good idea to have two or three shades, in black, gray, and possibly blue or any other medium tone. This is useful when you are marking a canvas for stitching in light colors, where the black marks might show through. If your colors are predominantly deep, you can use the black marker for the entire design. When they are very light, use gray which shows well as you are working but won't show in the finished work. The medium-colored markers are for medium shades and aren't quite as important as you can substitute the gray instead.

Canvas is sold like fabric, by the yard, and comes in rolls which are cut to the length you want. The sides are more tightly woven than the rest and are called selvedges. Whenever you are working with a canvas, it's best to use it with the sides on the right and left, not the top and bottom, so be sure the canvas is wide enough to accommodate the design completely, leaving at least $1\frac{1}{2}$ inches of unworked canvas around the stitched area. If your canvas is much wider or longer than you need, cut it down to a more manageable size and put masking tape around the raw edges. To tape easily, use the $1\frac{1}{2}$-inch or 2-inch width, cut off the length that you need, and place it, sticky side up, on a table. Put the edge of the canvas on the tape so that half

Marking a design on needlepoint canvas.

the width of the tape is covered. Smooth it onto the tape and then fold the rest of the tape around the canvas to the other side and smooth it down. Other adhesive tapes will also work, but cellophane tape won't stick to the canvas so don't bother with it. Whenever you can, leave 2 inches around each side of the design area of plain canvas; then, if you need to add an extra row or two of stitches when the work is finished, you'll have plenty of room. If you cut the canvas so that the selvedges are cut off, mark the top so that the canvas is held with the sides on the sides as you mark the design. This is

necessary as there may be a slight variation in the weave of the canvas from side to side and top to bottom. Even when the canvas is just the right size, leave the selvedges at the sides and tape the top and bottom, which will be raw as they have been cut from a large roll and will catch the yarn as you stitch if left untaped.

Place the design on a table and put the canvas on top of it to see how it fits. Look at the design and see whether it is easy to follow all the outlines. If so, you can proceed. If not, tape the design and canvas to a sunny window or place them on a glass table and place a light under-

A needlepoint design that was stitched on a canvas marked with outlines and colored with acrylic paints.

neath and you'll see everything. Start to mark the canvas by drawing the outlines of the entire work. Then, take the ruler and mark the exact center of the stitched area. Lift the canvas and mark the center of the design in the same way. A small dot or cross is sufficient; this mark is used as a guideline to align the canvas and the design should either move as you work, or to realign them when you check on your progress by lifting the canvas.

Then outline the design itself. Draw the largest outlines first. When they are complete, draw in the details. Every now and then lift the canvas and check to see that you have included all of the design. Place a sheet of paper between your hand and the canvas as you lean on the canvas so that you don't smudge it.

If you like to work with a paintbrush, you can use India ink instead of felt-tipped markers. If you don't want to get ink on the design, place a sheet of clear plastic between it and the canvas and paint the outlines with a thin brush, starting at the top of the canvas and working down. When you have finished, leave the canvas

where it is until it is completely dry. The ink can smear quite easily while it is wet but once it dries, it's waterproof.

Coloring the canvas is largely a matter of preference. Many find it is the best way to work, while others prefer to color the design and follow it as a guide while they stitch. If you are using a lot of different colors you may find it easier to stitch when the canvas itself is colored in beforehand. To color a canvas you can use acrylic paints, oil paints, or waterproof markers. Each has its merits. The acrylic paints are simpler to use than oils; you can wash them off your hands and they don't require turpentine. To use acrylics, thin them with the medium that is available, not water, as it will soften the canvas. Then, using as little paint as possible, carefully fill in the outlines of your design as indicated by a colored version of the paper design. Make sure that the paint does not clog the spaces in the canvas, making them unstitchable. Allow each area to dry before starting the next and then let the entire canvas dry overnight.

If you use oil paints, thin them with turpentine, not linseed oil as is usually recommended for painting; the linseed oil may leave a residue on the canvas. Place the canvas on a sheet of clear plastic if you don't want to ruin the paper design. Then paint in the outlines as you would with acrylics. Let the canvas dry for at least twenty-four hours.

When you can find truly waterproof markers in enough different colors, they are probably the easiest to use to color a canvas because they dry almost instantly. When you have filled in the entire design, it's still wise to let it dry overnight before you start to stitch it; but there is no danger of a marker filling in the spaces on a canvas.

Needlepoint charts are an entirely different way of stitching a design. When you use a chart, you draw only the basic outlines of the project on the canvas and then you follow a graphed version of the design to stitch. In marking the canvas, you'll find it helpful to divide it into four equal sections by drawing two lines, from side to side and top to bottom, crossing in the center. If the canvas is fairly large, you can draw six lines, dividing it into sixteen equal sections, using the basic outlines as a guide to draw the lines within. This will help you as the chart is made on graph paper, filled in with symbols that stand for colors in the design. In general, each square on the chart represents one stitch on the canvas, and you work from a chart by stitching in the color indicated by the symbol in the corresponding square. In many cases the predominant color or the background is shown on the graph by blank squares, so that when you see them, you know that these are stitches that you will make even though the squares look empty. The symbols are depicted on an area outside the chart, showing which color each symbol stands for.

The charts can be quite good to work from as you don't need to mark the canvas beforehand, but many people feel that they can lose their place too easily when they look away from the chart to make the stitches. To remedy this, use a pencil and cross out the stitches on the chart as you do them; that way you will always know exactly where you are just by looking at the chart and your canvas. Another bit of confusion that sometimes occurs when using charts from various sources is that the textured stitches are sometimes included in the color charts. In this case one square will represent one stitch, but the stitch may cover more than one space on the canvas. However, charts of this nature are identified as such so that you will know what to do.

You can make your own chart on graph paper, provided that it has enough squares to encompass your entire design. Otherwise you will have to tape pieces of paper together or do the design on several pieces. Choose the symbols you plan to use and write them down so that you don't forget which color each stands for halfway through your chart. Outline the stitched area on your canvas and count the number of mesh, or canvas threads, on each side. Mark off the same number of squares on the graph paper. Enlarge the design so that it and the graph paper are the same size and their outlines are the same. Then mark a symbol to correspond to each color section in the design until the entire design has been transferred from the enlargement to the graph paper. If you tape the design to a window or onto a glass table, you can put the graph paper on top of it and fill the symbols in within the outlines of the design as you see them through the paper. This won't work under usual lighting conditions as the graph paper is rarely transparent enough to see through.

An interesting part of planning a chart for a needlepoint work that has been inspired by a mosaic is that the mosaic itself may serve as your chart, with slight changes due to the change in medium. If you can get an enlargement of the mosaic itself without losing clarity, you may be able to follow it as if it were a chart by drawing the intersecting lines across the center. Then mark the canvas and place it on the enlarged mosaic. If necessary, hold them up so that light can filter through and you can see the tesserae of the mosaic. Count the number of

A canvas that was outlined and stitched following a chart. As the results are the same, the method chosen is a matter of personal preference when both a drawn and charted version of a design are available.

mesh, or crossing threads in the canvas, that go into each of the pieces in the mosaic. If they are uniformly sized throughout the work, you can then follow the chart by making that number of stitches for each tessera in the mosaic. In some mosaics the central figures are made up of smaller chips, so check each area carefully. In other works the tesserae may be placed at an angle to each other, creating a narrow, wedge-shaped space between each one. In this case you can fill in these areas with stitches as needed. You can't leave any unworked threads in a needlepoint canvas.

Deciding when to use a chart and when to mark the canvas is up to you, based on your own method of stitching. Many people prefer to mark the outlines of a design on the canvas; the entire design is then in view at all times and you can stitch it without referring back and forth to a chart. This technique also tends to make the work more portable; you need only the canvas, a needle, and the yarn to do your needlepoint.

Charts are usually better for complex designs that include details of single stitches in different colors. The single stitches are clearly indicated on a chart, each stitch has its own square, and these are nearly impossible to indicate on a canvas with a marking pen. It is for this reason that finely detailed needlepoint designs are most often presented in chart form. The charts are precise and when followed correctly produce exact results.

Where lines meet on the canvas there is often some question as to which color area a particular stitch falls into. A design with larger shapes will look fine whichever section you put a single stitch into, but you can see how placement might affect the outcome when each stitch has a definite position in a detailed pattern. Thus, your own working techniques and the complexity of the design are the deciding factors. Make the choice that seems best to you and you'll be sure to enjoy doing mosaics in needlepoint.

CHAPTER FIVE

The Basics of Needlepoint

IF YOU'VE NEVER DONE needlepoint before, you'll be pleased to discover how much you can do with a minimum of equipment, for needlepoint requires only canvas, yarn, and needles. This simplicity of materials is one of the appealing features of this kind of stitchery.

Canvas is the foundation of your needlepoint. It is usually white or pale shades of beige or ecru. Linen and cotton are widely used to make canvases, which are woven so that openings form between the threads as they cross each other. The weave is balanced, which means that there are the same number of threads up and down and from side to side in 1 inch of canvas. Because weaving is done with the up-and-down (or warp) threads under tension, there is a slight variation in the actual canvas. That's why you always stitch with the sides of the canvas at the sides of your design, rather than at the top and bottom. In referring to the size of the canvas the term *mesh* is used. The mesh is the number of threads per inch, as measured from side to side. The threads themselves are always counted, not the spaces between them. The usual range of

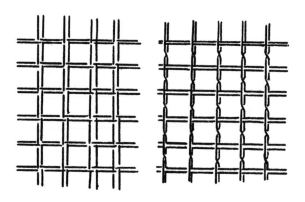

Penelope weave

Twisted warp thread, penelope

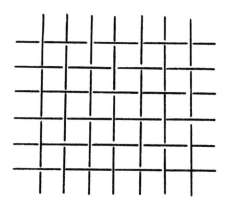

Mono weave

Needlepoint canvases, with the penelope weave on the left and the mono weave on the right.

sizes is from 3 to 26 mesh per inch. The larger-mesh canvases are often called rug canvases and have between 3 and 5 mesh per inch. In needle-point, work done on these canvases is some-times called quickpoint, as the stitching goes very quickly. The next range of sizes, from 6 to 8 mesh per inch, is used for gros point, which means "large stitch" in French. The range from 8 through 14 is the most widely used and, when a designation is made, is often referred to as needlepoint canvas. The higher-numbered mesh, from 15 up, are called petit point, "small stitch," as that is exactly what they are. You may find that different sources refer to the mesh sizes with different names, but the important fact is just how many mesh there are in 1 inch.

Mono canvases are woven so that there is a single thread at each intersection. They are widely used because the threads are easy to count and stitch. Penelope canvases are those woven with double threads at each intersection. When you look at a penelope canvas, you may see a double number as the mesh size, such as $^{10}/_{20}$. This is because you can use the canvas both ways. As you stitch over pairs of threads in a penelope canvas you use it as you would a 10-mesh mono canvas, and if you push the threads apart with your needle as you stitch, you can use the canvas for petit point, resulting in the equivalent of 20-mesh-per-inch mono canvas. This feature is quite helpful in working mosaic-inspired needlepoints; you can work the central figures in the smaller stitches and the background and border in larger stitches, just as many mosaics are made with two sizes of tesserae. If you plan to use a canvas this way, check when you buy it that the threads push apart easily. There is a type of penelope canvas in which the top to bottom threads are twisted as the canvas is woven; they are impossible to work this way. The twisted-thread penelopes occur most widely in the rug-weight canvases; they are made this way to strengthen the canvas for a rug.

In general, you will find that the central range of sizes of mesh is available in both types of canvas, mono or penelope. The larger-mesh canvases are usually penelope and the finer ones are mono. Whichever you choose, be sure that the canvas is smooth and free from lumps, knots, and irregular threads. Any canvas with these flaws will give inferior results and is cer-tainly not suited to your stitching standards.

Canvases come in many widths, the most usual being from 24 to 40 inches, with the finer canvases in somewhat narrower widths and the rug canvases somewhat larger, up to 60 inches. Always buy canvas wide enough to leave a margin around the stitched area for assembling and blocking. If you are planning several proj-ects, you can use the canvases for them, so that you need never worry about buying too much canvas. You'll always be able to use it in the future. Another possibility is to buy the widest canvas, such as a $^5/_{10}$ penelope which can be as wide as 60 inches, and use it for several articles. This way, you are being economical and making the best use of the canvas. Buy the fine-quality canvases; the ones of lesser quality are no bar-gains.

The mesh that you choose is largely depen-dent on what you are planning to make and to some extent on your experience in needlepoint. The finer canvases take longer to complete, as there are more stitches in every inch. Gros point canvases are faster but are usually penelope and harder to learn to do the stitches on if you don't already know how. A 10- or 12-mesh mono canvas is a good one to start with. You can learn the stitches easily and the canvases are well suited to many articles that you will make.

Yarns are bought to go with the type of canvas you have chosen. The most widely used fiber for needlepoint is wool, with good reason. It is the longest-wearing, best-looking, and easiest to work with. You invest a lot of time and planning in your needlepoint and, as in the canvases, you'll be better off in the long run with the best wool yarns. Generally, there are two types of wool yarn used in needlepoint. One is Persian, made up of three strands which can be sepa-rated for use on finer mesh. The other is tapes-

Needlepoint yarns.

try yarn, made up of four plies, or strands, tightly twisted together; it should be used as is. When you separate the three strands of a Persian yarn, you'll see that each individual strand is made up of two plies which should not be separated. Persian yarn is widely used and you can adapt it to fit many canvases by using more or fewer strands. The relationship between the yarn and the mesh is an important one. For attractive results, you want the yarn to fit smoothly into the spaces of the canvas, covering it well. If the yarn is too thin, the canvas will show through and your stitches will look flat. If it is too thick, it will push the mesh apart and you'll find that, after a while, the stitched area is so bulky that you won't be able to stitch around it. The right yarn is one that allows the stitches to form nicely while covering the canvas completely. A chart depicting the most widely used canvas, yarn, and needle sizes follows the section on needles in this chapter.

For the larger-mesh canvases use rug wool or the specially made quickpoint wool. This type of yarn is always used as is, since you cannot separate the strands successfully. If you need to, you can double the yarn. If it is still too thin, you can use several strands of Persian yarn or perhaps doubled tapestry yarn instead. Rug yarns are often made in synthetic fibers but they really don't work well in needlepoint and should be avoided if possible.

When you go to buy yarn, you'll find that it is sold in different quantities. In good needlepoint shops you can buy Persian yarn by the strand, about 18 inches long, which serves two purposes: it is the ideal length to use for stitching (the yarn will fray if it is too long), and when you are stitching a complex design, you can buy an incredible number of different colors in the small amounts you will need. Persian yarn is also sold in skeins with pull-out centers so that the yarn unwinds from the middle of the skein out. This keeps it in better condition than if it is unwound from the outside in. These skeins are usually 25 or 40 yards long, or 4 ounces in weight, depending on how the manufacturer

labels his yarn. A similar yarn, also sold in skeins and on cards as well, is crewel yarn. Crewel yarn comes in two strands which you can separate; it looks just like a lightweight version of Persian yarn. It is thinner and can't be used interchangeably with Persian yarn even though it looks almost the same when you see it wound in a skein. Of course, you can try it out and use it by adding a strand if needed.

Tapestry yarn is most often sold in 40-yard skeins and can be used in the same work as Persian yarn if you are careful to balance the two, seeing that they cover equally and that the tapestry yarn is not too thick for your canvas. The weight of the yarn does vary from one manufacturer to the next, so you should try it on a piece of the canvas you're using to see if it fits. Tapestry yarn is also sold in hanks, or large circles of strands. If you are going to use one of these for needlepoint, you should open the circle of strands out to its full size and cut right through the yarn, spreading the strands somewhat. This will give you lengths of yarn that are good for stitching.

Rug yarn is sold in skeins and hanks, usually by weight. Quickpoint yarn is often sold in 40-yard skeins. Both of these yarns are fairly limited in their range of colors, so you may be better off using several full strands of Persian or tapestry yarn instead if variety in hue is part of your design. You can also combine the yarns in a project by stitching them on an extra piece of canvas beforehand to see that they are well balanced.

Special effects can be made by using the polished look of perle or pearl cotton in small areas. It is fairly thin, so you'll need to use several strands at once. Other lustrous effects can be achieved with metallic yarns or silk threads, but these can be tricky to work with. You can experiment with many yarns once you're used to how the stitches are done and what will work in needlepoint. One non-needlepoint yarn to stay away from is knitting yarn, which tends to be less durable and will fray while you stitch.

Needles used in needlepoint are called tapestry or needlepoint needles. They have blunt tips and large eyes so that you can thread them easily. Choose the needle to go with the yarn and mesh size, so that the yarn fits in the eye of the needle and the mesh aren't pushed apart as you stitch. The largest size, used for rug-weight canvases, is called a rug needle, size 13. The other sizes range from 15 to 24; the larger the number, the smaller and narrower the needle. The medium range, from 18 through 20, is most widely used, with the higher numbers being reserved for petit point.

The following chart depicts the combinations of canvas, yarn weight, and needle sizes that work well together:

Needlepoint needles.

Mesh	Yarn	Needle
3	rug yarn, doubled	13
4	rug yarn, three full strands of Persian yarn	13
5	quickpoint yarn	15
6	two full strands of Persian yarn, two strands of tapestry yarn	15
8	four strands of Persian yarn (sometimes five)	16
10	three full strands of Persian yarn, one strand of tapestry yarn	18
12	two strands of Persian yarn (sometimes three)	18
14	two strands of Persian yarn	20
18	one strand of Persian yarn	22
20	one strand of Persian yarn	24

As you can see, there is always some variation possible in the yarn that will be best suited to a particular project. That's why most needlepointers make a small sampler with the planned stitch, yarn, needle, and canvas before they begin the actual project. That way they know just what to do on the design canvas without risking any surprises.

Yardage requirements for yarns should be estimated before you buy any yarn for your project.

Yarn is dyed in lots and skeins may vary a bit, even when they are the same shade. When you look at a yarn package label you'll see a number, letter, or combination of the two, which is the dye lot of that particular skein. Make sure that all the skeins of yarn in any one color you buy are from the same dye lot. It's also important to buy enough yarn to complete your project. Many times you'll find that you can't match the dye lot later on if you need more yarn. It is hard to give a general rule for how much yarn you'll use; each stitch has a different requirement. The continental or tent stitch is used for many works and, as an example, uses about $1\frac{1}{2}$ yards per square inch of Persian yarn in a full strand on 10-mesh canvas. To find out how much you would need for an entire work, multiply the width by the length and then multiply by the number of yards used for the stitch in a square inch. In this example, on an 8-inch by 10-inch canvas, you'd need 120 yards of Persian yarn: $8 \times 10 = 80$; $80 \times 1.5 = 120$. When you are using several colors, estimate how many square inches each color takes up. Be generous in these estimates; you can use leftover yarn in many ways and it's better to have an ample amount to finish your article. When you need only small amounts of yarn, try to find a store that sells it by the strand. Also, the salespeople in good needlepoint shops will be knowledgeable enough in most cases to estimate how much yarn you'll need.

When you don't have any idea how much yarn a special stitch will use, make a sampler on the same size canvas, using the same kind of yarn in a measured amount. Stitch a square inch and write down how many yards of yarn you used to complete it. (Remember to include the yarn left in the needle that is too short to stitch, as this will occur in the project as well.) Multiply that amount by the number of square inches in the project.

Other equipment you will use in your needlepoint includes two pairs of scissors—one to cut the canvas and a smaller pair of embroidery-type scissors to cut the yarn and snip out any incorrect stitches—masking tape for the canvas edges, and a thimble if you like to use one. Sometimes a frame is recommended to hold the canvas as you stitch, but it is really not necessary and can make some stitches actually harder to work. You should also set up a place in which to keep your supplies so that they are organized. You can use a drawer, a large basket, or any other receptacle that will hold them. Keep your needles in a pincushion or a cork. Don't leave them in the canvas when you aren't working on it; they will not always stay put. Also

A

B

Whether bought by the strand or cut from a larger skein, strands of a single shade should be knotted together with a loose overhand knot in the center to keep them from tangling or being mixed in with other strands of a similar hue. A. Single strands knotted. B. Strands folded in half before knotting.

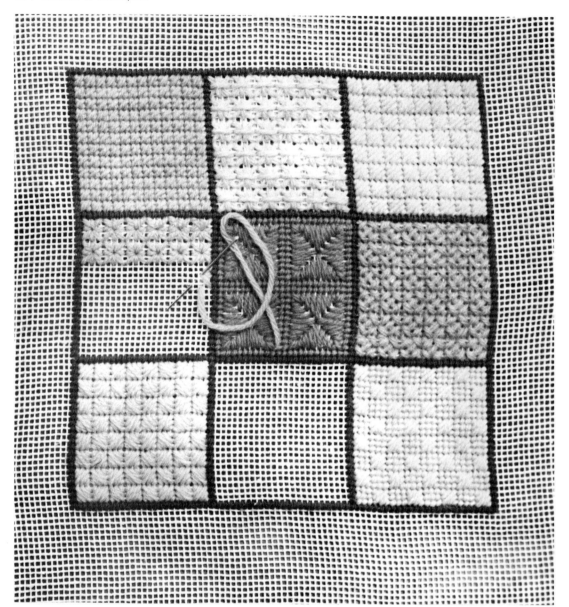

Stitching and filling in an area in a sampler design.

keep your scissors in a safe place, not loose in a workbasket where you might place your hand on their tips by mistake. When you are using yarn that comes by the strand or that you have cut into strands from a hank, tie loosely in groups of the same color with a knot in the center. That way you can be sure that similar shades aren't confused with each other and the strands don't get tangled. When you have extra yarn not being used for the current project, put it in a box or drawer and store it away from bright light, which might make the colors fade.

Keep your design ideas and sketches with your other materials and you'll always know where to find them.

Where to start, once you have your materials assembled and your design set up: in needlepoint designs with central figures or other small features, begin to stitch by doing the smallest parts first. This is done so that you can see them easily and can do them before the larger areas of color obscure the canvas. For example, if you are stitching a figure with an outline, do the outline first, as it will often cover only one mesh intersection with one stitch along the outline. If you were to do the inside color and the background, the single mesh would be very difficult to stitch. The same is true for small areas, so start with the smallest parts and stitch each consecutively larger section. If there are central figures, complete them all before starting the background. The border is usually stitched last, if there is one.

Generally, when stitching an all-over pattern, start in the upper right-hand corner and work

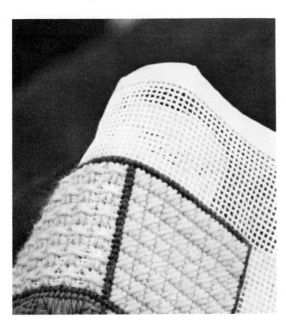

Masking tape along the edges of a canvas as it is stitched.

out and down from there, using several needles with the different colors of yarn so that you don't have to thread the needle anew each time the color changes. If some repeating feature in an overall pattern is smaller than the others, stitch all of the units of that feature first and then do the rest of the pattern in order of size. An exception is when you are using a combination of very light and dark colors. Stitch the light ones first, as they would pick up some dark fibers if done after the dark areas. The basic aim is to do the design in the easiest way possible. You'll find that your own method of working will develop as you stitch.

To thread the needle, hold it in your right hand and wrap the end of a cut piece of yarn around the needle with your left hand. Hold the yarn around the needle with your thumb and forefinger, as close to the needle as possible so that it is almost touching your fingers. Then slip the needle out while continuing to hold the yarn so that the yarn forms a small loop right in front of where you are holding it. Slide the eye of the needle over the loop and between your finger and thumb so that the loop protrudes from the eye of the needle. When it is large enough to grasp, let go of the yarn, reach to the other side of the needle, and pull it through. Your needle is ready for stitching.

To start the yarn on the canvas in needlepoint, hold it at the back of the canvas and work the first few stitches around it to secure the end. You must never make knots in needlepoint; they cause lumps on the right side of the finished work. Once you have done several stitches around the yarn and it is held in place, cut off the tail that is hanging down so that it doesn't tangle with your needle or yarn as you continue to stitch. When there are already stitches on the canvas, start a new piece of yarn by sliding the needle under the backs of the last few stitches in the area; this holds the yarn in place.

To end off the yarn, take it to the back of the work and slide the needle into a few of the

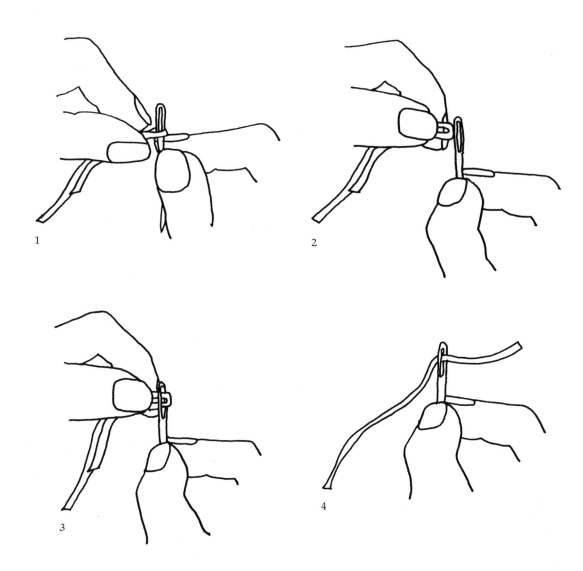

Threading a needlepoint needle.

stitches on the back. Cut it off right next to the canvas. Each time you start and end the yarn in needlepoint, cut off the ends that hang down at the back of the canvas as close as possible to avoid tangling, which can become impossible to rectify. Leaving tails of yarn on the wrong side of the work is so simple to avoid that there's no excuse for letting it happen on your canvas.

Tension in stitching is an important part of how well your stitches turn out. You are aiming for a balanced tension throughout the work which creates smooth but plump stitches. When you pull the yarn too tight it gathers the mesh together and the stitches look flat. If it is too loose the stitches will get caught in one another as you make them and just won't look right. If you are learning the stitches, the proper rhythm will come to you with a little practice. A sampler worked in different colors is a good way to learn new stitches. You can make each area as large or as small as you wish; the results are often quite attractive, and you'll learn many stitches as well.

To hold the canvas while stitching, roll it toward the wrong side, starting at the left. To stitch, hold the rolled canvas in your left hand, leaving the area you are stitching exposed, and stitch with your right hand. (If you are left-handed, reverse the order.) Even when you're working on the center of the canvas, it's easier to hold the canvas if you roll up the remaining part. Just be sure that you keep the rolled section out of the way so that you don't catch it with the needle as you stitch. As you begin to work you'll find that the canvas is not pliant, because of the sizing that is added to the canvas. The sizing will soften as you work, making the canvas more flexible. Many people bend a new canvas several times before beginning to stitch to make it softer and easier to handle.

Turning the canvas is necessary for many stitches. As you turn the canvas to do the next row in this type of stitch, work each row in exactly the same manner so that the stitches form evenly. Make sure that you turn the canvas all the way, so that the top is at the bottom,

and then the top is at the top again. In working small areas it's not hard to get confused. The canvas looks the same and you might accidentally turn it only to the side. To avoid this problem, write the word *top* on the top or otherwise mark it so that you know just where it is at all times.

Fixing mistakes in needlepoint is not difficult, particularly if you see them right away. The best thing to do if you have made the wrong kind of stitch or used the wrong color is to remove the thread from the needle and use the needle to pull out the wrong stitches, one at a time. When you are finished, take the yarn to the back of the canvas and end it off. Start with a new piece of yarn, even if it is the same color. Once you've stitched with a piece of yarn and then pulled the stitches out, it will be in no condition to be reused. You may see some of the yarn still caught on the canvas after the stitches are out and you should pull these fibers off the canvas before you start to stitch again.

If you've made a fairly large mistake, you can use embroidery scissors to cut the stitches from the wrong side of the canvas. Be very careful; it's all too easy to cut one of the mesh as you cut the yarn. Whenever possible, pull the stitches out one at a time. If you do cut the yarn, do as little as necessary and undo the rest. Then work the ends of the cut yarn into the backs of several stitches.

Patching the canvas can be done if you do cut a mesh or two in error. It's best to use a patch instead of trying to add in one new canvas thread, which can be tricky. If there are stitches in the area, undo them until you have about 1 square inch of unworked canvas. Then cut 1 square inch of canvas from the identical canvas of the project. If you have no extra canvas that is the same, use a corner of the 2-inch margin. Canvases of the same size from different sources may vary; this is why you must use the same one for the patch. As you cut out the patch, mark its sides with a dot of permanent ink. Then place it on the wrong side of the canvas,

Holding a needlepoint canvas rolled up as you stitch so that it is easier to reach the area being stitched.

making sure that the sides are parallel to the sides of the canvas. Line up the mesh on the patch and the canvas, stitch through both layers with the stitch and color intended for that area of the canvas, and you'll never know it was patched after you've covered the entire area with stitches.

Piecing canvas sections is done when you are stitching a large project for two reasons: either your canvas is not wide enough to accommodate the entire design, or it is easier to handle the work in sections and then to sew them together when all of them have been completed. In the first case, piece the parts together before you start by cutting off the selvedges on the side of each piece of canvas. Then overlap the two sides for about $1\frac{1}{2}$ inches and match up the mesh. To hold the sections in place as you stitch, you can baste them with strong white sewing thread and work the needlepoint right over the basting. This type of join usually does not show, but it's better to use a wider canvas if at all possible.

To work in sections, plan the design so that there is a logical place to join the sections, for example, a rug stitched in six equal squares with borders around each of the squares as an integral part of the design. When all sections are stitched and they have been blocked, fold back the margins and stitch the sections together with the same color yarn as the outermost border. Carefully stitch back and forth, aligning each mesh of one section with the corresponding one on the opposing section. To avoid having canvas visible, you may find it helpful to stitch an extra row all the way around the sections and sew them together one stitch in from the edge so that the extra row actually folds to the wrong side when you are finished. This method generally won't work without the borders; when a solid color meets in two sections the stitches you use to sew them together are usually too visible.

Blocking is done when you have completed the entire needlepoint project. Many stitches pull the canvas out of shape because they slant. If you have made an entire canvas with the continental stitch you might have trouble blocking it back to its original shape in one step, so repeat the blocking. Sometimes you'll discover that other stitches have caused very little distortion, but you should block in any case. You'll need a board on which to stretch and tack the needlepoint, so it should be strong enough to take it. A 3-foot by 5-foot sheet of $\frac{3}{4}$-inch plywood is an ideal blocking surface, and you will use it over and over again for many projects. Be sure that one or both sides of the plywood have been sanded or they may snag your yarn. The board must be large enough for the entire stitchery, margins and all. If you don't plan many large projects, you can get a smaller sheet. Other materials that you can use are pressed boards or even an old clean pastry board that you don't mind sticking tacks into. You'll also need some rustproof pushpins or tacks, heavy paper, and your waterproof markers.

Outline on the heavy paper the shape of the canvas as it was before you began. Use a right angle or a T square to make sure that you draw the corners at a right angle. Then tape the paper outline onto the board. Place the stitched canvas on the board. If it has a great deal of texture, block it face up. If you've used the continental, basket weave, or other uniform stitch, block the piece face down. You can also block face down for the other stitches, but the process will flatten them to some extent. Start by aligning one corner of the canvas with one corner of the shape drawn on the paper. Push in a tack, outside the stitched area but not so close to the edge of the canvas that it can pull through the masking tape and tear it. Then line up the next corner, put in a tack, and fill in the entire side between the two tacks with more tacks, spaced about 1 inch apart. Now you're ready for the pulling if your work is distorted. Go to the remaining corners and pull each one as close to the corresponding corner on the paper as you can. Tack it in place and tack along the side that is parallel to the

Blocking a finished needlepoint canvas. The outer, unworked canvas margins are stretched as necessary to achieve the correct shape in the stitched area itself.

first one you did, pulling on the canvas as you go so that it meets the line drawn on the paper as closely as possible. With some works, this will be difficult and it sometimes takes two people—one to pull and the other to tack. If you can't get it right up to the line, do it as nearly as you can. Then tack down the two remaining sides, pulling if necessary.

Take a clean towel and wet it. Place it on top of the canvas and use a steam iron, or a regular one, to press the towel lightly, creating more steam. As you move the iron along, lift it up and set it down on the next spot; don't slide it as if you were actually ironing. When you're sure that all areas of the stitchery have been steamed, remove the towel and let the needlepoint dry for at least twenty-four hours. Make sure that it is bone dry before you remove it from the board or it will spring back into its unblocked state.

When your work is badly distorted, repeat the procedure. If the second blocking doesn't straighten it out completely, you may be better off mounting the work so that it appears square, by including some of the stitched area in the seams or other mounting procedures. This rarely occurs unless the entire needlepoint was stitched in the continental stitch, which for this reason is not recommended.

Mounting your blocked needlepoint is done according to what you have made. If you have made an article that will be framed, it's often best to have it mounted professionally by someone who has worked with needlepoint articles before. The same is true for slippers, pocketbooks with frames, and upholstery. Almost everything else can be mounted at home.

Pillows are most easily sewn on a sewing machine. You can choose many different types of backing for the pillow, depending on the setting in which it will be used. Velvet is one of the most popular pillow backings. It adds a lot to the work, especially when the hue of the velvet picks up one of the stitched colors. Linen, corduroy, canvas, even suede or leather are all suitable as well; any sturdy fabric can be used. To sew the pillow, cut out the backing so that it is the size of the stitched area plus 1 inch on all sides. Trim the canvas margins to 1 inch, snipping off the corners so that they are no more than $\frac{1}{2}$ inch wide at each corner diagonally above the stitched area. If your pillow is round, now cut the canvas, as all shapes are worked on square or rectangular canvases and trimmed after blocking. Place the backing fabric face down on the front of the needlepoint and pin it in place. Stitch on the machine using a strong needle and thread, leaving one side open so that you can put the pillow form or stuffing into the pillow after you turn it right side out. Then stitch the opening by hand, using thread in a matching color. Whenever you sew needlepoint, stitch one row of stitches in from the edge of the stitched area so that the canvas doesn't show through. If your canvas does show, you can add a few stitches using the yarn of the project even after the work has been sewn.

Some needlepoint articles should be lined, as the exposed canvas edges will begin to fray with use. You can use lining materials such as taffeta, or any lightweight fabric that goes with your project and its intended use. Sew the lining and the needlepoint as you would any material lining, making sure that you work just within the edge of the needlepoint. You can always make your own lining by measuring the needlepoint area and adding 1 inch to each side for an instant lining pattern. Whenever you make an article of clothing that includes needlepoint, such as a vest, be sure to line it for the long wear it will surely deserve.

Tassels and fringe are sometimes added to needlepoint with good results, but they tend to distract the eye and should be used sparingly.

For other suggestions on how to assemble needlepoint, check the specific projects. They are descriptive and may give you many ideas that you can adapt for your own works.

CHAPTER SIX

Needlepoint Stitches

NEEDLEPOINT STITCHES ARE depicted in stitch diagrams which are precise representations of what you do on the canvas to form the particular stitch. As you look at a diagram you'll see that it is drawn on graph-type paper, which is intended to show the mesh. The stitch itself is then drawn just as you will see it when it is correctly stitched on the canvas. To make the diagram easier to follow, numbers are added to show where the needle goes into the canvas from front to back and where it comes to the front from the back to continue the stitch. In this system the odd numbers always stand for the back-to-front motion, and the even numbers, for the front-to-back. As you look at the diagram it appears that you must do each step to correspond to a number, one at a time. Some needlepointers do like to work this way, with the work in a frame and one hand poised below and one hand above to pass the needle from front to back and to the front again. However, it's faster and usually easier to do many of the stitches in a series of motions that often comprise two of the steps on the diagram. To do this, bring the needle to the front or right side of the canvas to begin a stitch. Then continue the stitch by sliding the needle into the canvas at the proper spot and along the back of the canvas and out to the front again at the proper

place, all in one motion. For most stitches you can continue to work in this manner, ending one stitch and beginning the next in one pass of the needle. This creates the rhythm of needlepoint and you'll find that the more you do, the more relaxing it is as it becomes instinctive and you no longer have to concentrate on how to make the stitch. Some stitches are worked from right to left and some from the bottom up, the top down, left to right, or diagonally. Yet they are all simple to learn and fun to do. The variety in how each is made adds to the excitement and makes it possible for right- and left-handed people to be equally at home doing needlepoint.

To learn any stitches you don't already know, follow the diagrams carefully and check with the photographic examples and you can't go wrong. Whenever you can, try sliding the needle along the back and doing each even-to-odd step in one motion. You can in almost all stitches, with the exception of the very first step, which is always to bring the needle to the front of the canvas in the appropriate spot.

Compensating stitches are used in the more complex stitches to fill in areas that cannot be covered with the whole stitch. For example, if a stitch covers three mesh and your design limits it to two mesh, work just that one stitch over two mesh in the same method and direction as

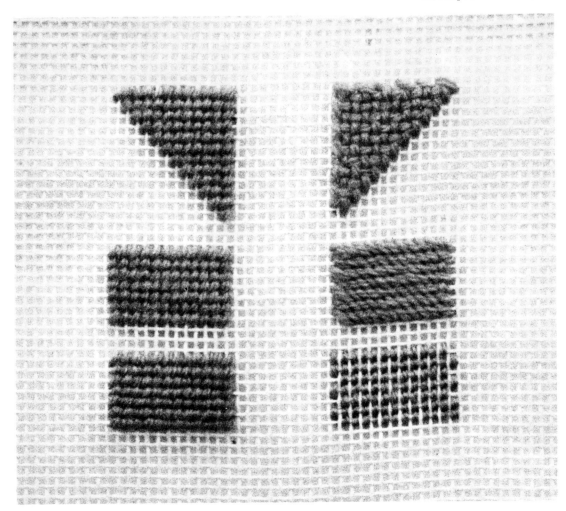

The basket weave, continental, and half cross-stitches, shown with the right side, or front, of each stitch on the left and the wrong side, or back, on the right.

if you were able to complete the stitch fully. This makes it possible to use ornate stitches anywhere in your design. The compensating stitches are shown in the diagrams whenever they are hard to figure out. In many cases they can even be replaced with the basic stitch without changing the appearance of the design very much.

The *tent stitch family:* These stitches are the basic stitches in needlepoint. Many designs are made using only these stitches, with color changes providing the pattern. Although each stitch is done differently, all are in the same group because they all have the same appearance on the canvas when seen from the right side. It is only when you see them from the back that they look different.

The *basket weave stitch* is perhaps the most useful of the tent stitches, as it hardly distorts the canvas. Just as it sounds, the back of the stitch looks as if it were woven when the stitch is done correctly. This stitch is sometimes called the diagonal tent stitch. Follow the diagram to place the first stitch in the upper right-hand

Basket weave stitch.

corner. If you're left-handed you may prefer to work from the lower left; you can follow the diagram by turning the book so that the stitch appears to have been done that way. For all subsequent even rows the stitch moves up diagonally on the canvas, and for all subsequent odd rows it moves down. This also makes the stitch easier to work. Once you get the idea of how it is done, you never need to turn the canvas as you stitch. With the exception of the final stitch at the end of each diagonal row, which is done to start the first stitch on the next row correctly, a tip for doing the basket weave stitch is to remember that when you are stitching the even rows, which move up on a diagonal, the needle points to the left-hand side and is parallel to the top and bottom of the canvas as you do the stitch. On the odd rows, which move down, the needle points to the bottom of the canvas and is parallel to the sides. A mistake frequently made when learning this stitch is to leave off either the last stitch in one row or the first stitch in the next, so always check to be sure that you have done them. When you leave out a stitch it is confusing and can throw off your rhythm. Whenever you need to stop stitching, complete a row of basket weave so that you will begin again at the top or bottom. If

you stop in the middle of a row, you may forget and go back in the same direction without completing the row. Although this stitch seems complicated at first, it's well worth learning.

The *continental stitch* is done in horizontal rows, and you turn the canvas around from top to bottom at the end of each row. Then you work the next row and turn the canvas back to its original position. If you look at the wrong side of the continental stitch, you'll see a series of slanting stitches, created by the motion of the needle as you slide it along the back of the canvas to form the stitch. This stitch is quite handy for small areas where the basket weave is too complex to work, but it shouldn't be used for large areas as it does distort the canvas. It can also be done vertically, from top to bottom; again, you turn the canvas at the end of each row.

The *half cross-stitch* is the third of the tent stitches. It also looks the same from the front, but from the back it looks like a series of short, vertical stitches. To do it, work from left to right and then turn the canvas so that each row is done from left to right. This stitch should always be done on penelope canvas as it slides under the mesh in mono canvas and just doesn't stay put. As you do the half cross-stitch, re-

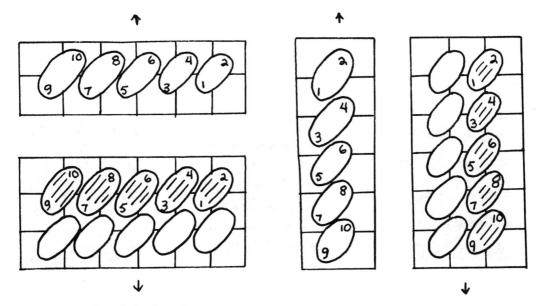

Continental stitch, horizontal version.   Continental stitch, vertical version.

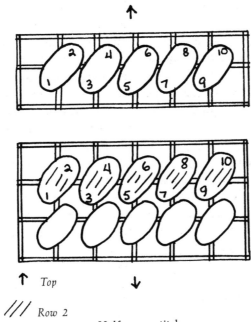

↑ *Top*   ↓

/// *Row 2*

Half cross-stitch.

Gobelin stitches: upright, slanting, and encroaching.

member that the needle always points down and you'll do it correctly.

Gobelin stitches are made so that each stitch covers more than one mesh intersection, unlike all of the tent family stitches, which always cover one intersection on the right side of the work. The Gobelin stitches are simple to do. They are used in many combinations to make textured pattern stitches, so you'll find them an essential part of your needlepoint repertoire.

The *upright* or *straight Gobelin stitch* is worked so that it covers two or more mesh vertically, as the name tells you. It is usually worked from left to right without turning at the end of each row, but rather coming back from right to left. The back of each odd row and each even row will look different, but the front will look the same. Some people prefer to stitch from right to left and turn the canvas at the end of each row, but it's up to you.

The *slanting Gobelin stitch* is a slanting stitch that can be worked in many heights and degrees of slant. Going up two mesh vertically and over one horizontally in each stitch is one effective version of this stitch. It also can be worked from left to right and right to left, or always right to left by turning the canvas.

The *encroaching Gobelin stitch* is done so that the top of the stitch in the second row goes around the same mesh as the bottom of the previous stitch. It can be done in upright or slanting versions and from left to right and then right to left, or by turning the canvas, from right to left on each row. Just be sure that you don't catch the previous stitch with your needle as you do it.

Pattern stitches are those that form a definite texture in the finished work. They are quite decorative and can be used for accents, or in different areas of the canvas in endless combinations. Many of them require compensating stitches to fill in an area completely, as some don't cover the canvas as well as others. It's a

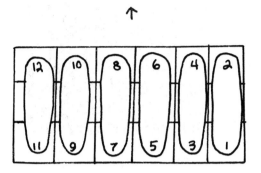

Upright Gobelin stitch.

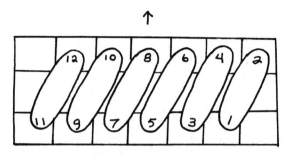

Slanting Gobelin stitch.

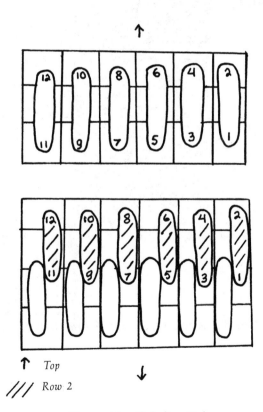

↑ *Top*

/// *Row 2*

↓

Encroaching Gobelin stitch.

Pattern stitch sampler, outlined with the continental stitch, vertical and horizontal.

Cross	Upright cross	Long-armed cross
Two colors Hungarian One color	Knotted	Parisian
Jacquard	Turkey Loops uncut	Diagonal cashmere / Cashmere
Diagonal mosaic	Old Florentine	Oblique Slav
Brick		Byzantine Many colors

Chart showing the location of each stitch in the sampler.

good idea to make up a sampler of stitches to see just how they work and select the ones you like. When you see that a stitch doesn't cover the canvas completely, work it in light colors or tint the canvas before stitching in the same color if you are using a deeper shade.

Cross-stitches are done in two parts. Start the stitch at the left and work the first half of the cross to the right. Then cross the stitches on your return to the left. The next row is worked in the same manner so that all of the stitches cross in the same direction.

Upright cross-stitches are stitched one at a time, from right to left, turning the canvas at the end of each row. When you have completed an area, you can fill in the tiny spaces left between each

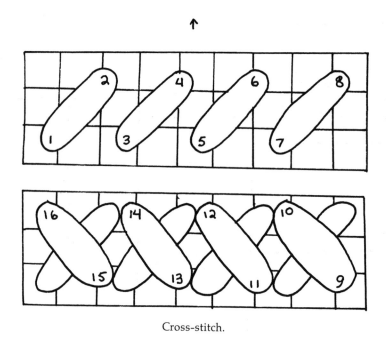

Cross-stitch.

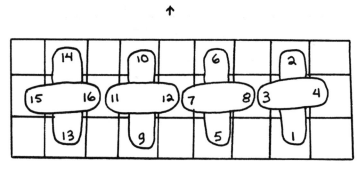

Upright cross-stitch.

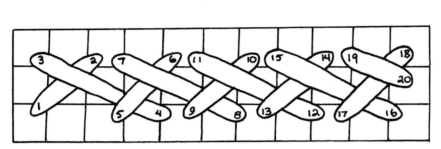

Long-armed cross-stitch.

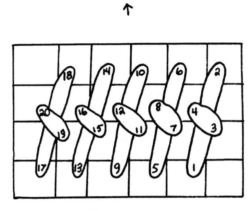

Knotted stitch.

stitch at the top, bottom, and sides with one-mesh compensating stitches.

Long-armed cross-stitches are worked with a longer stitch and more slant to each half of the cross. They are worked from left to right, turning the canvas at the end of each row, and they produce a lovely texture.

The *knotted stitch* is basically a long slanted Gobelin, tied down with a shorter stitch with an opposite slant. Work it in one step for each stitch, from right to left, and turn the canvas at the end of every row.

The *Hungarian stitch* is worked with a space between each stitch, which is composed of a short, a long, and a short upright Gobelin stitch,

filled in by the stitches in the next row. Each unit is always made up of three stitches; stitch from right to left on the first row and then left to right on the next. Using different colors of yarn for the even and odd rows makes an interesting effect. When you've completed an area, fill in the remaining mesh with compensating stitches of whatever height you need.

The *Parisian stitch* is quite similar to the Hungarian stitch; however, there are no spaces left between the stitches. The stitch is basically one short, one long, one short, one long upright Gobelin, all the way across the row, which is worked from right to left and then turned. On the following row the long stitches fill the

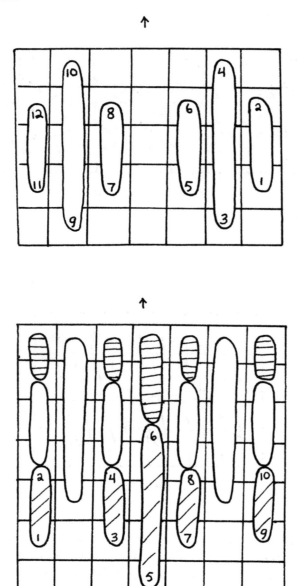

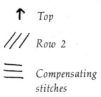

↑ *Top*

/// *Row 2*

≡ *Compensating stitches*

Hungarian stitch.

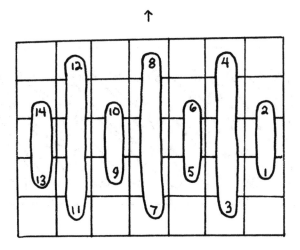

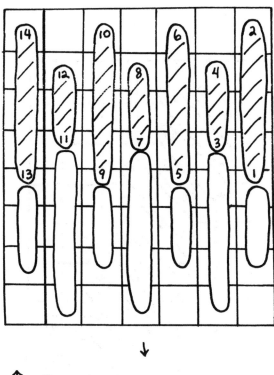

↑   *Top*

///   *Row 2*

Parisian stitch.

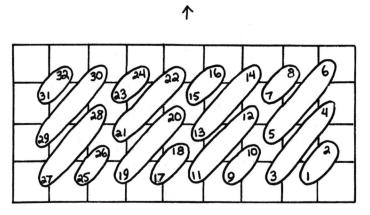

Cashmere stitch.

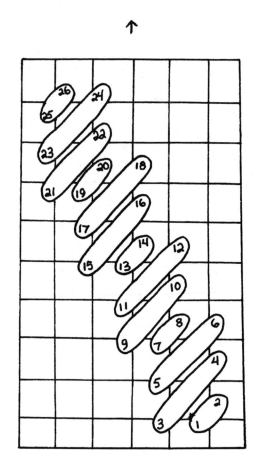

Diagonal cashmere stitch, first row.

spaces left by the short stitches in the previous row. Always work fill-in stitches for this stitch; the first and last rows don't cover the area because of the variation in height of the stitches.

The *cashmere stitch* is a stitch made up of rectangular units. It consists of a tent stitch, two slanting Gobelin stitches, and a tent stitch, worked over each other in sequence to form the units. It seems easiest to work from right to left, but from the bottom of the area up to the top. Then turn at the end of each row and stitch from right to left again.

The *diagonal cashmere stitch* is a variation that is done by stitching from the bottom up, on a diagonal. Stitch the first unit as for the cashmere stitch and then create a diagonal by stitching the next two slanting Gobelin stitches just to the left of the last tent stitch so that each unit shares a stitch with the previous one. It forms an interesting angular stripe.

The *diagonal mosaic stitch* is done just like the diagonal cashmere with only one slanting stitch, so that you repeat one small, one large, and one small, one large slanting stitch up the canvas from lower right to upper left.

The *Byzantine stitch* is also worked from the

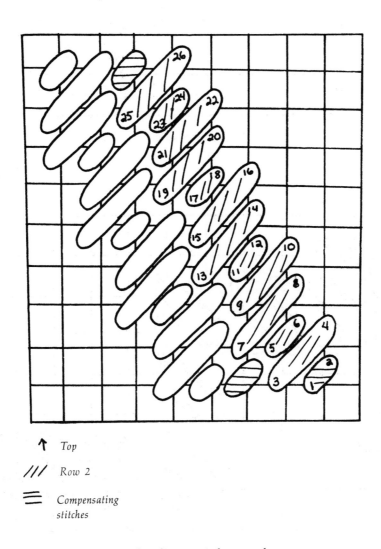

↑   *Top*

///   *Row 2*

≡   *Compensating stitches*

Diagonal cashmere stitch, second row.

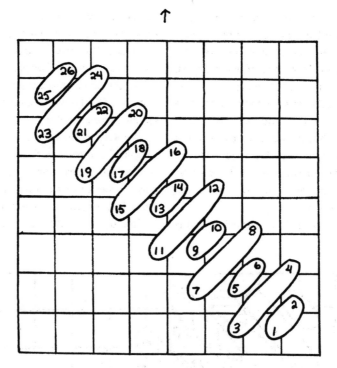

Diagonal mosaic stitch.

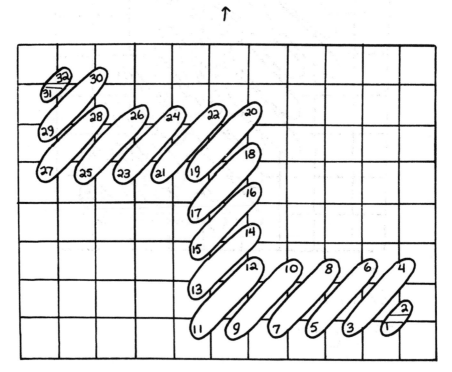

Byzantine stitch, first row.

lower right to the upper left, in a series of slanting Gobelin stitches formed in a regular pattern like steps. Compensate at the beginning and end of the series of stitches with one tent stitch. Cut the yarn and start at the bottom again each time until you've filled half the area. Then turn the canvas and start at the lower right and work in the same way to fill the rest.

The *Jacquard stitch* is a variation on the Byzantine stitch in which each row of slanting Gobelin stitches that is completed is followed by a row of continental tent stitches. These stitches are beautiful when each row is done in a different color but is otherwise worked as usual.

The *old Florentine stitch* is a long and short stitch, worked in sets of two long and two short, from right to left. The canvas is turned, and on the next row the long stitches fill the spaces left by the short stitches in the previous row. It should be used on articles that don't get a lot of wear, as the stitches are easily caught and pulled, so it is fine for wall hangings. On the first and last rows you'll need to add some compensating stitches to fill the spaces.

The *brick stitch* is simple but effective and makes a good background. It is an upright Gobelin stitch worked up two mesh and down two mesh each time so that it forms a wavy line; the

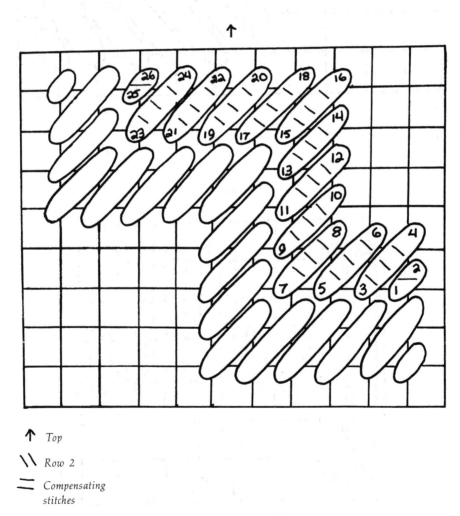

↑ *Top*

\\ *Row 2*

= *Compensating stitches*

Byzantine stitch, second row.

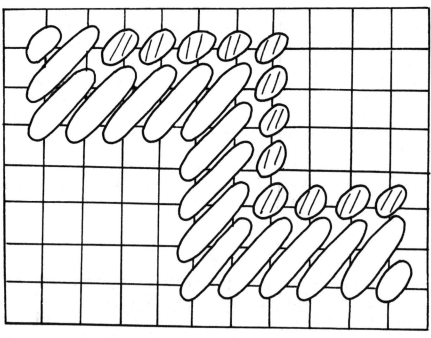

↑　*Top*

/// *Row 2*　　　　　　　　　　Jacquard stitch.

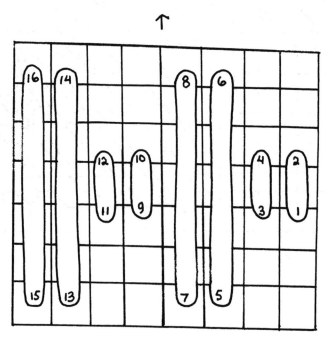

Old Florentine stitch, first row.

next row fills in the spaces. The brick stitch is worked from right to left and then the canvas is turned. Filling stitches are needed at top and bottom.

The *oblique Slav stitch* also should be used on things that are relatively untouched upon completion; it also has long stitches that might snag. It is basically a very slanted Gobelin stitch, worked from left to right; the canvas is turned after each row. The extreme slant makes it look quite nice when it's completed. Use a shorter stitch to begin and end each row of stitches.

Turkey stitches form loops that can be cut open to make pile, as on a rug. They are worked from the bottom, from left to right, cutting the yarn at the end of the row and starting again. It's easy to cut the yarn on this stitch as each one locks itself into place. It is mainly a backstitch,

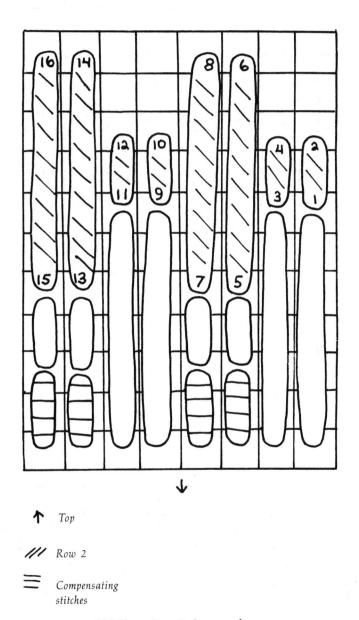

↑   *Top*

///   *Row 2*

=   *Compensating stitches*

Old Florentine stitch, second row.

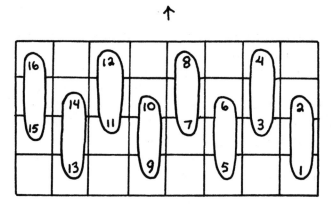

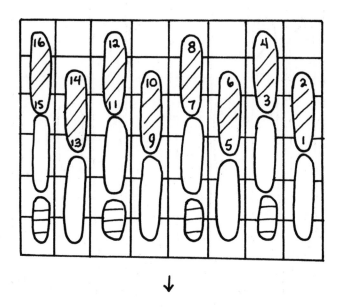

↑   *Top*

///   *Row 2*

=   *Compensating stitches*

Brick stitch.

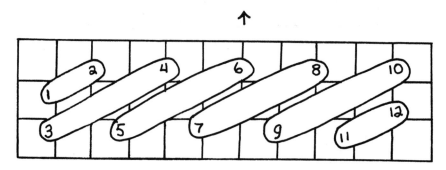

Oblique Slav stitch.

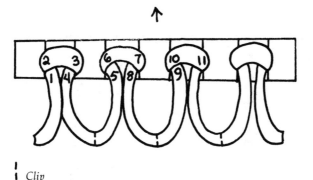

Clip

Turkey stitch, which is worked from the bottom up.

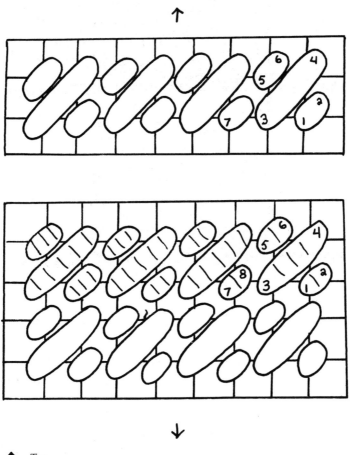

↑ Top

＼＼ Row 2

Mosaic stitch.

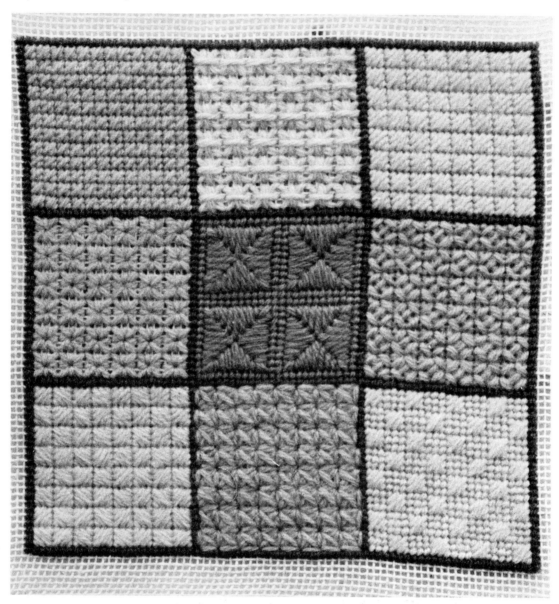

Sampler of stitches that are uniquely suited to a mosaic effect.

worked between the mesh. You can guide the length of the loops with your thumb as you make them. When worked closely and cut, this stitch makes a pile that is as deep as you make each loop in size. Any design with turkey stitches in it should always be blocked face up with the tufted turkey area left unpressed if possible.

Stitches uniquely suited to a mosaic effect are those formed in square units. You can use them with a true mosaic effect by making various-color stitches in these units to form a tiled wool design.

The *mosaic stitch* is most aptly named. It is a small, square unit formed with one tent, one slanting Gobelin, and one tent stitch. It is

Mosaic	*Smyrna* *cross*	*Scotch*
Algerian *eye*	*Triangle* *squares*	*Crossed* *corners*
Reversed *scotch*	*Outlined* *cross*	*Scotch* *checkerboard*

Chart showing the location of each stitch in the sampler.

worked from right to left and the canvas is turned at the end of each row. The small squares it makes are open to much experimentation in mosaic-inspired patterns.

The *Scotch stitch* forms a larger square. It is made up of five stitches in each unit, with the largest forming the center diagonal of the square. It is done from right to left, turning canvas at the end of each row.

The *reversed Scotch stitch* is also called the checkerboard stitch. It is worked with the Scotch stitch, except that each unit is stitched with the opposite slant so that they form a new pattern when placed next to each other. On following rows work the stitches by turning the canvas and being sure that you are reversing the stitch's slant under the previous stitch as well.

Scotch and continental checkerboard is stitched by forming a series of Scotch stitch units, leaving a one-mesh space between each. These spaces are filled with continental stitches. The procedure may be reversed as some prefer to do the outlines first.

The *Smyrna cross-stitch* is made up of four stitches, crossing first on the diagonal and then horizontally and vertically. Make the entire stitch at once, working from left to right and starting the yarn again on the left each time. The important thing to remember here is that all the stitches must be crossed in the same way for a uniform effect.

The *Algerian eye stitch* is interesting, if only to theorize as to what the name means. It forms a square as you make eight spokelike stitches, all

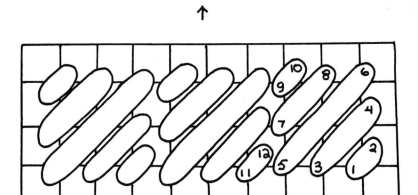

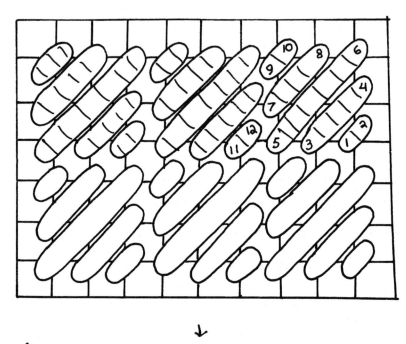

↑ *Top*

↘ *Row 2*

Scotch stitch.

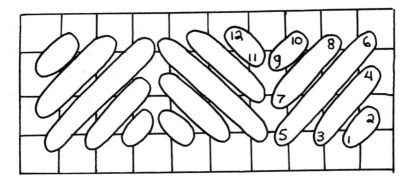

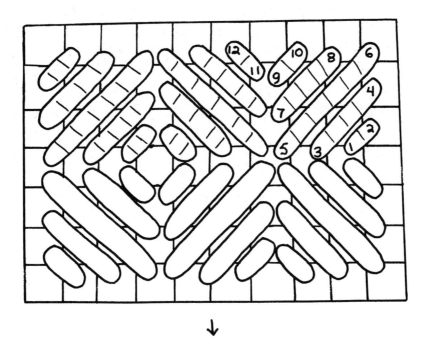

Reversed Scotch stitch.

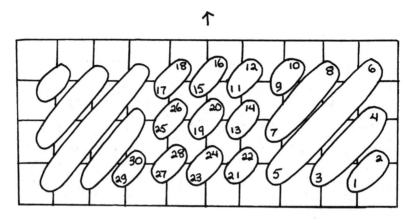

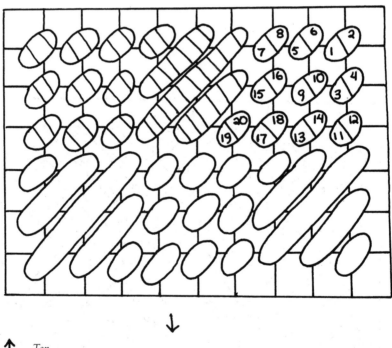

↑   *Top*

⟍⟍   *Row 2*

Scotch and continental checkerboard.

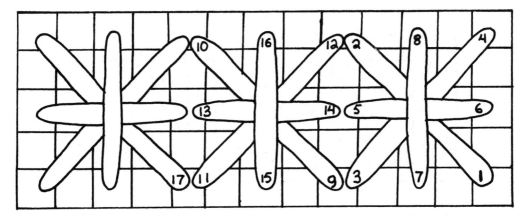

Smyrna cross-stitch.

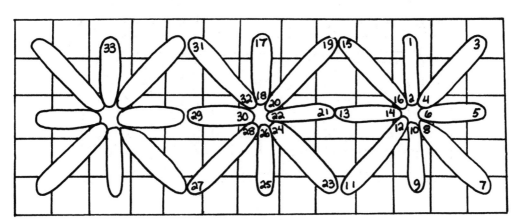

Algerian eye stitch.

going into the center of the unit. You should work the spokes in the same order in each unit for the best results. You can work the stitch in either direction and turn the canvas, or cut the yarn and start again. It doesn't cover the canvas entirely, but you can tint the canvas beforehand or add small stitches to fill in if you prefer. You might also try doing the stitch in light colors.

The *Italian* or *outlined cross-stitch* is worked from right to left; turn the canvas for each row. Complete each unit, making the cross-stitch first and then the outline. Always be certain that the cross and outline are made in the same manner for each stitch unit.

Triangle squares are stitch units that cover quite a large area. You can work them right next to each other or with spaces that you later fill with continental stitches. For a bold design, use different colors.

Cross-corners stitch is just that—a cross-stitch that has smaller stitches crossing each of the points of the diagonal stitches that make up the

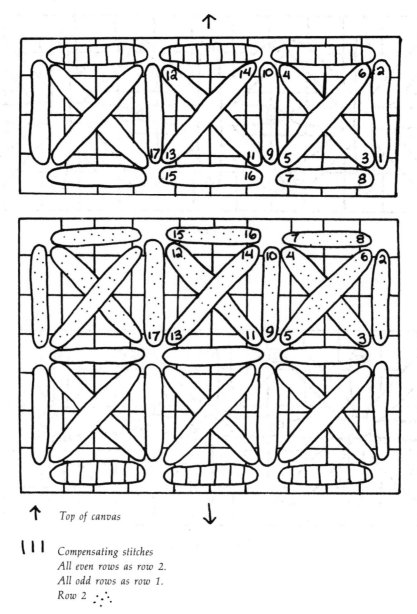

↑　*Top of canvas*　↓

|||　*Compensating stitches*
All even rows as row 2.
All odd rows as row 1.
Row 2 ∴∴

Italian or outlined cross-stitch.

cross. Work the cross-stitch itself first and then the crossing corners, making each unit separately. The stitch is sometimes done in two colors, but in this case it loses its square effect.

Stitch variations are subject to endless experimentation by the avid needlepointer. You'll find that you can even make up your own, once you know the basics and some of the more textural pattern stitches. They will enhance your mosaics in needlepoint as you learn to do and enjoy them.

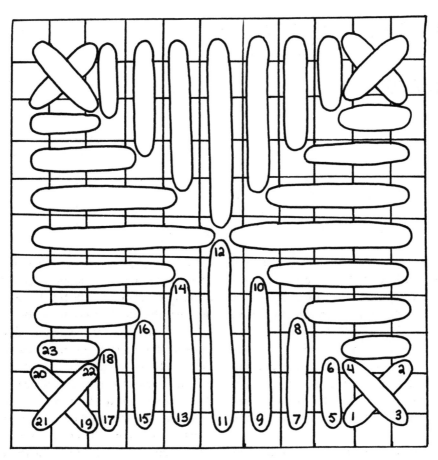

Work first two sides as shown, then turn canvas, or turn partway for each side.

Triangle squares stitch.

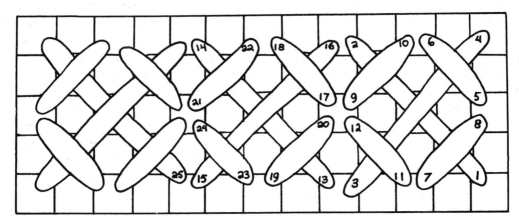

Crossed-corners stitch.

CHAPTER SEVEN

Projects

NOW YOU'RE READY to create your own mosaics in needlepoint. The following projects will give you an idea of how many exciting ways you can use needlepoint to beautify the articles that you see and use every day.

The materials that you'll need to assemble your projects are usually found in the home and are easy to work with. For almost all projects the basics are: sewing needles, scissors, and thread; a sewing machine if you prefer using one; white glue that dries clear; a ruler; paper and pencils to check pattern sizes; waterproof pens; masking tape; and felt, which is a great all-purpose lining material that can be cut to shape and often is glued in place, as it doesn't unravel or fray when cut.

Many interesting projects include the use of found objects that are given a new life through needlepoint. They are all around you, just waiting to be discovered and recovered. The pleasure of deciding what you want to do first is equal to that of finding a design that you'll enjoy stitching in your new style of needlepoint.

Pocket Crest

An extremely effective way to add a spark of color to a basic blazer or jacket with a patch pocket is to make a new, needlepoint pocket with an unusual design. Interesting patch pock-

ets in many patterns may also be added to garments without existing pockets and to denim clothing of all sorts with terrific results. You'll find that the possibilities are endless. The pelican motif shown here was designed for a jacket but would be equally effective on other clothing that would be suitable for a patch pocket. The design is adapted from the Noah's Ark panel, the section where the birds are entering the ark, found in San Marco, Venice. Along with the usual materials, you'll need a piece of 10-mesh mono canvas, 8 inches by 8 inches, a piece of taffeta or other suitable lining material of the same size in a shade that goes with—or matches—the color of your garment, and Persian yarn in the amounts given.

Make the pattern according to the size of the pocket. The pattern can be easily made by carefully removing the left-hand breast pocket. Working from the front of the jacket and using a pair of pointed embroidery scissors, pull the pocket away from the jacket, exposing the threads that hold it in place. Snip through several threads, one at a time, and pull them out. Undo the entire pocket, removing any loose threads that are left on the jacket.

Place the pocket on a sheet of paper, leaving its seam allowances folded back, just as they were when you removed it from the jacket. Draw around it, so that you have an outline on paper of the exact shape and size of the pocket.

NAPKIN RINGS.

BLOTTER ENDS.

PLANTER.

CLOCK FACE.

TENNIS RACQUET COVER.

Pocket crest, worked in a full three-strand Persian yarn on 10-mesh mono canvas.

Then draw another outline $\frac{1}{2}$ inch wider all around, to allow for the natural contraction of the needlepointed canvas that occurs as you stitch. Transfer this outline onto your canvas and be sure that you have at least 1 inch of unworked canvas all the way around it. The design should generally conform to the size and shape of the pocket you are using. As this design has a solid background, you can use it as is by centering it on the outlined shape and adding or subtracting from the background for the needed size and shape.

After you have outlined your canvas, tape any raw edges and stitch the central figure of the design as indicated on the chart. Fill in the background as needed to fit your pocket, using the basket weave stitch to minimize warping of the canvas. When you have finished the stitching, check the size by placing the original pocket, with its seam allowances still folded back, face down on the right side of the canvas. You should be able to see about two mesh of stitching all the way around the pocket so that you can sew it in place on the jacket without any unworked canvas showing.

Block the needlepoint. When it is dry, cut out the pocket shape from the canvas, leaving about $\frac{3}{4}$ inch around the stitched area. Cut out the lining fabric to match. Place the needlepoint and the lining together, faces in. Sew around the edges just inside the needlepointed area, leaving about 3 inches along the top seam open so that

Drawing of the original pelican design, as adapted from the Noah's Ark panel in San Marco, Venice.

Simplified version, modified to suit the canvas, which can be transferred to your canvas instead of using the chart.

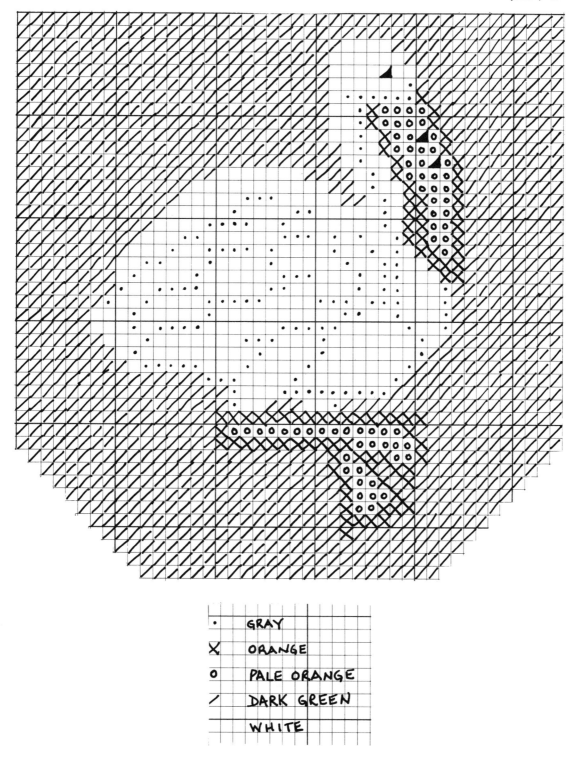

•	GRAY	
X	ORANGE	
O	PALE ORANGE	
/	DARK GREEN	
	WHITE	

Chart of the pelican, stitched in basket weave and continental stitches. By the strand, the yarn required is: dark green background, 15; pale orange, 3; white, 5; gray, 3; yellow, 1; brown, 1.

you can turn it right side out. If you sew by hand, use the backstitch; on a machine, use moderate pressure and 8 to 10 stitches per inch. Turn right side out, making sure that all corners are fully extended. If necessary, press lightly with a warm iron on the lining side to flatten the seams. Fold in the opening and blindstitch in place by hand so that the pocket is a complete unit. Pin it in place on the jacket through the lining. Make sure that the new pocket is in the same place as the original one. Sew it on around the sides and bottom with a strong, lightweight thread such as silk, using a tiny blindstitch so that the sewn joining isn't visible.

When you are adding a pocket to a garment that had no pocket or working with another article of clothing, follow the same procedure as for the jacket pocket. When adding a new pocket, always try on the garment with the pocket pinned on, before sewing, to be sure that the alignment and placement are correct. The addition of a needlepointed patch to any garment will mean that it should be dry cleaned by a cleaner who has experience working with needlepoint and can handle it correctly. But you can remove the pocket if you prefer to wash the garment itself by hand or in a machine.

Planter

You can make an attractive, functional planter in needlepoint, using a 2-pound coffee can as a liner. The design structure and assembly procedure would also be effective for smaller or larger cans to make cheerful planters, desk ac-

Planter, one side, stitched in a full three-strand Persian yarn on 10-mesh mono canvas.

Planter, other side.

cessories such as pen and pencil catchalls, and—if you leave the top rim of the can exposed so that the plastic lid that came with the can can still be used—canisters with hundreds of uses.

The theme of reeds, lily pads, and pond with a hazy, tree-lined shore in this design is derived from a French Art Nouveau work done in the 1890s. As 2-pound coffee cans are of standard size and shape, the dimensions given are correct. If you're working with another size, measure carefully and use the standard procedure to form the right size needlepoint pattern area. You'll need felt for the outside bottom of the can, a small can of clear polyurethane and a brush, a piece of 10-mesh mono canvas 21 inches by 10 inches, and Persian yarn by the strand in the amounts shown.

To prepare the coffee can, wash it out and let it dry completely. Then coat the inside with several coats of clear polyurethane. Other waterproof varnishes can be used if you have them on hand, but the polyurethane seems the most durable. Be sure to cover the inner rim and side and bottom seams well and let them dry between coats. This will prevent rusting when the plant is in place.

Mark the outlines and the design on the canvas, cut it to the overall size, and tape any raw edges. Stitch the design and block.

When the canvas is dry, trim the extra canvas to 1 inch. If that is the amount you left around the stitchery, merely remove the masking tape. Place the needlepoint face down and miter the upper right-hand corner by folding it down to the back of the stitches so that you can just see the corner stitch. Then fold down the top canvas allowance and the right side allowance and baste in place through the canvas only where the top and side meet at the mitered corner. Place the can on its side on the stitched area so that the top of the can just meets the top of the needlepoint. Lift the left side and roll it around the can. Glue the unworked canvas to the can along the left-hand edge with white glue. Use a

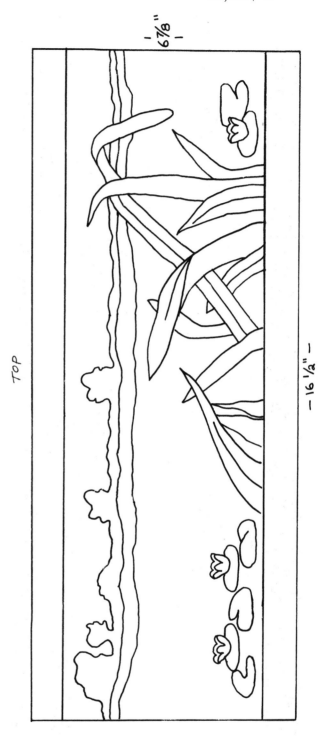

Drawing of the planter design, derived from a French Art Nouveau work, to be enlarged to the dimensions shown for direct transfer to the canvas.

TOP

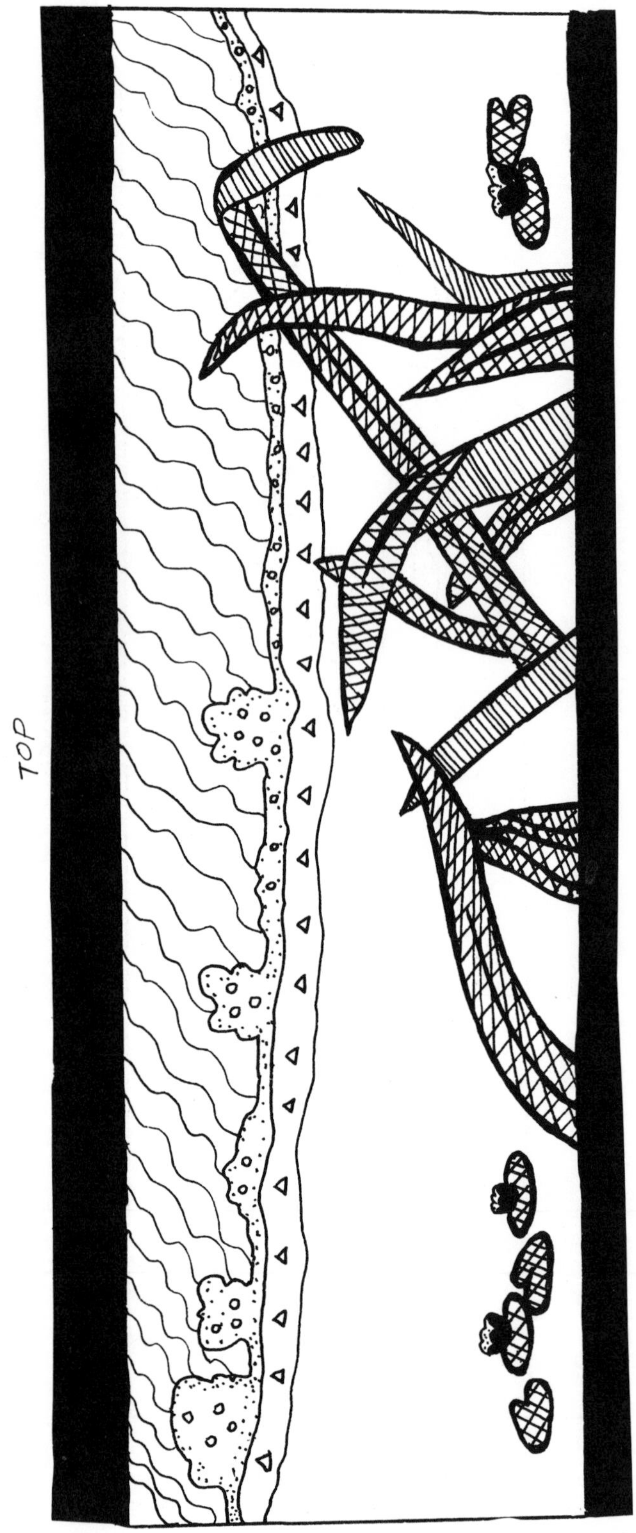

Diagram for color placement, for use with the drawn canvas.

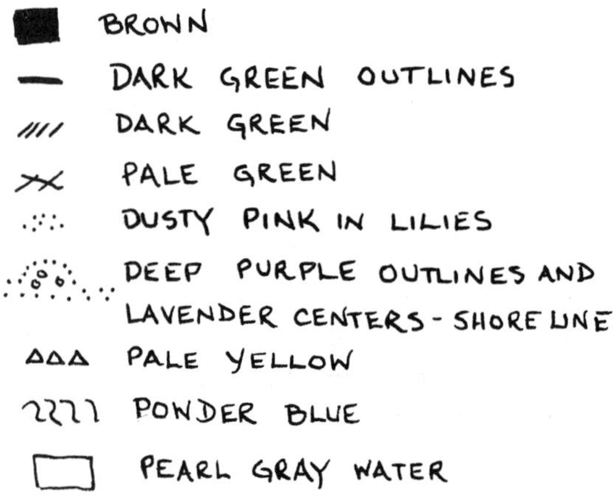

BROWN

DARK GREEN OUTLINES

DARK GREEN

PALE GREEN

DUSTY PINK IN LILIES

DEEP PURPLE OUTLINES AND
LAVENDER CENTERS - SHORE LINE

PALE YELLOW

POWDER BLUE

PEARL GRAY WATER

piece of masking tape to hold it in place until it has dried completely.

Remove the tape and bring the right side up to the glued section. With a sewing needle and strong thread, carefully sew the two sides together where they meet, working stitch by stitch from the top down, as invisibly as possible. When you reach the unworked canvas at the bottom continue down and stitch it together. If you still have a workable length of thread, leave it there. Glue the unworked canvas to the bottom of the can, forming V-shaped pleats as needed. Use the extra thread to sew the pleats in place. While the glue dries, cut out a felt circle the same size as the bottom of the can. Spread a thin coat of glue on the felt and smooth it in place on the folded canvas and bottom of the can. Let dry.

To use the planter you can slip in a potted plant or fill the bottom of the can with an inch or so of gravel or pebbles to allow for drainage. Then put the potting soil and plant directly in the planter.

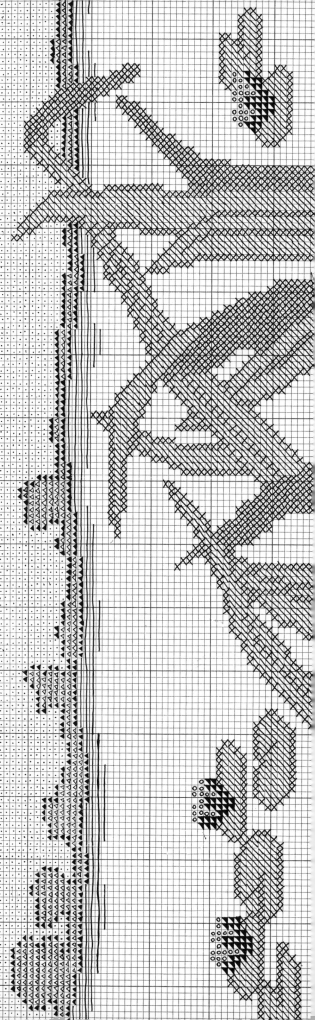

·	POWDER BLUE	MOSAIC STITCH
	PALE GRAY	PARISIAN ST
■	DARK BROWN	BRICK ST.
◣	DARK BROWN	TENT STS.
X	OLIVE GREEN	"
/	PALE GREEN	"
—	PALE YELLOW	"
△	LAVENDER	"
▲	PURPLE	"
⊙	DUSTY PINK	"

TOP

Chart showing colors and stitches used.
The amount of yarn required by the
strand is: pale gray, 32; brown, 30;
powder blue, 20; olive green, 18;
pale green, 16; pale yellow, 10; purple, 6;
lavender, 6; dusty pink, 2.

Scissors Case

A scissors case is a handy way to keep your embroidery scissors sharp and safe. The dimensions given fit most standard scissors, but if you need to alter the pattern you can do so easily as the overall design, which was inspired by an ancient Egyptian tiled wall, can be repeated to suit the size of your case. For the needlepoint, use a 10 mono canvas, about 12 inches by 10 inches. The lining should be the same size in a sturdy fabric such as cotton canvas or sailcloth. Use Persian yarn in the amounts and colors shown.

Enlarge the shape of the case and check to see if it fits your scissors. When you place them on the paper pattern, there should be about ¾ inch all the way around the scissors. If there is not, enlarge or diminish the size as needed, keeping the proportions constant.

The case is made of two matching needlepoint sections. Copy two outlines onto your canvas, placing the outlines so that the two pieces are on the same mesh at top and bottom.

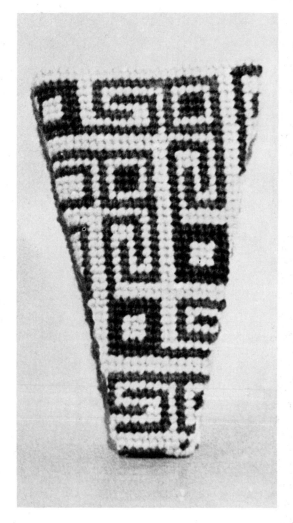

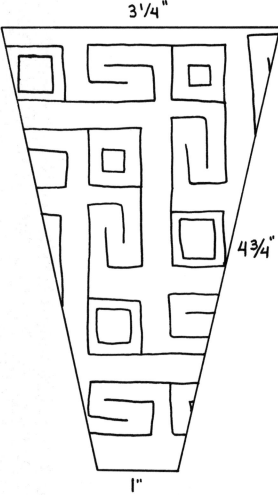

Scissors case, worked in full three-strand Persian yarn on 10-mesh mono canvas.

Drawing of the pattern, inspired by an ancient Egyptian tiled wall, with the dimensions of the case, which are to be outlined on the canvas twice, for the front and back.

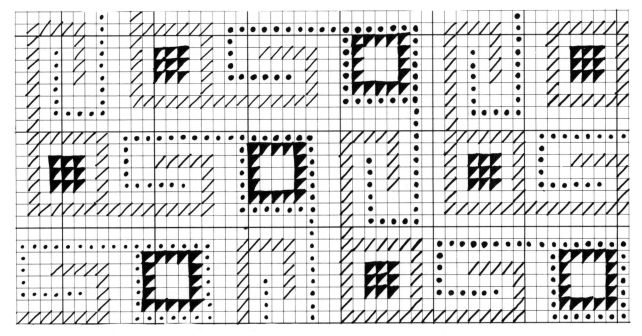

Chart of the repeating overall pattern, to be stitched in continental stitch. Yarn, by the strand, is: cream, 18; teal blue, 8; cherry red, 8; light brown, 4.

⟋	CHERRY	RED
◢	LIGHT	BROWN
•	TEAL	BLUE
	CREAM	

Leave at least 2 inches between the two shapes. When doing needlepoint on an oddly shaped area, always stitch on a square or rectangular canvas and cut it out after the blocking is complete. When the two outlines are marked, stitch the pattern using the charted design as needed to cover the area. Stitch the same pattern on the second piece. When both halves of the case are stitched, block the entire canvas.

Then cut out the two shapes, leaving about ⅝ inch all the way around each one. Cut out two pieces of fabric for the lining, using the needle-point as a shape guide. Place the two lining pieces face in and sew the two sides and bottom seams, leaving a bit more than a ⅝-inch seam allowance. Leave as is with the wrong side facing out. Place the two needlepointed sections together face in and sew the two sides and bottom seams just inside the stitched area. Clip

off the extra canvas at the two bottom corners so that they turn evenly and turn the case right side out. Slip in the lining. Fold in the top of the needlepoint and the top of the lining and slip-stitch in place. Place the case between two books or press lightly from the inside with a warm iron to flatten the top seam if necessary. Stuff one or two cotton balls into the bottom of the case to guard the points of your scissors, pushing them tightly in place with the blunt end of a pencil.

Paperweight

A needlepoint paperweight is a fine addition to anyone's desk. A very flat stone is used to provide the weight; you can find a suitable one just about anywhere—on the beach, in the

Paperweight, on 14-mesh canvas, stitched with two strands of Persian yarn.

country, or in a park. Try to find one that isn't more than $\frac{3}{4}$ inch thick; it can be more difficult to cover a very rounded stone. The one shown is oval, approximately $\frac{5}{8}$ inch thick, 4 inches by 3 inches in width and length, and conveniently flat on the bottom. The design is adapted from a motif in the stunning outdoor mosaic that covers the library building in University City, Mexico. The design is worked with a solid-color ground, so that you have leeway in the size and shape of the stone that you choose. The stone is covered with a 14 mono canvas; stitch with two strands of Persian yarn in the amounts and

colors shown. You'll need a piece that is large enough to cover your stone, with an allowance of about 2 inches of unworked canvas, and a piece of felt for the bottom of the covered stone.

Place the stone on a piece of paper and trace around it. Remove the stone and draw another outline, the same shape, $1\frac{1}{2}$ inches wider all around to allow for the wrap-around edges and the natural shrinkage that occurs as you stitch. Center the design on the paper outline where it looks best. Outline the canvas with the dimensions on your paper pattern and work with the canvas in a square or rectangle. Stitch the sun

Motif, freely adapted from the huge mosaic covering the outside walls
of the library building at University City, Mexico.

CONTINENTAL

PARISIAN

JACQUARD

Stitch diagram, showing placement of the Jacquard, Parisian, and continental or basket weave stitches.

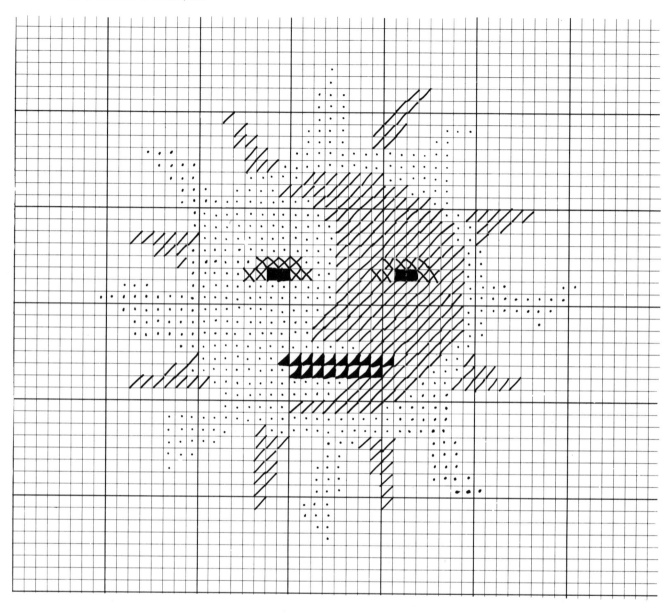

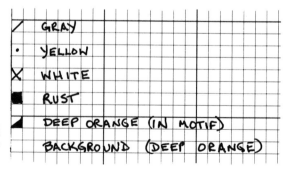

Chart, indicating colors, yarn needed, in 5.5-yard skeins, is: deep orange, 3; yellow, 1; gray, 1; yarn by the strand: rust, 1; white, 1.

and moon motif as shown on the chart and work the background as needed to fill your pattern.

To block the finished needlepoint, use a special technique so that the work assumes the shape of the stone as much as possible. Place your blocking board on a table or other flat surface and put the stone face up in the middle of the board. Dampen the needlepoint with a clean sponge and place it on the stone face up in the same position as it will be in the finished paperweight. Put in the tacks as usual, just outside the stitched area. When you have put in all the tacks, dampen the needlepoint a bit more and press lightly around the edges of the stone with your fingers to make the stitchery really conform to the stone. Allow it to dry completely.

Remove the dry, blocked needlepoint and cut the shape out of the canvas, leaving 1 inch of canvas all the way around the stitched area. Place the needlepoint face down and put the stone on the wrong side, so that it fits into the canvas as it was blocked. Cover the back of the stone with white glue. Pull the unworked canvas around to the back of the stone and smooth it into place, making V-shaped folds as needed. Thread a sewing needle with strong thread and stitch through the folds to hold the canvas in place on the back of the stone. Carefully turn it over, without disturbing the glued canvas, and place it on a sheet of waxed paper or aluminum foil to dry. While it is drying, cut out a piece of felt, following the original outline of the stone which you drew on the paper pattern. When the stone is dry, spread a thin, even coat of glue on the wrong side of the felt and smooth it in place on the bottom of the paperweight.

Wall Hanging

Wall hangings are one of the new forms that can enhance the walls of your home with vibrant mosaic-inspired designs. The design possibilities are limitless and are particularly interesting in the mythical figures of early Greek and Roman works. This one is an interpretation of the Personification of the River Jordan, found in the famous Ravenna mosaics. The canvas is a $5/10$ penelope, stitched with tapestry yarn within the figure, with the mesh carefully pushed apart so that the canvas is like a 10 mono; the rest of the design and the background are stitched with four strands of tapestry yarn using the canvas in its usual state, at 5 mesh per inch. To simplify the charts, two are given: one for the part stitched at 10 mesh per inch, which should be stitched first, and one chart for the 5 mesh per inch, to be worked when the first chart has been completed. The canvas should be 14 inches by 26 inches. You'll also need an equal-size piece of sturdy backing fabric; two rods for the top and bottom of the hanging—you can use decorative curtain rods, stained wood dowels, or Lucite bars, as long as they are at least 13 inches long; a cord with which you will hang the wall hanging from a hook; and wool tapestry yarn in the colors and amounts shown.

To stitch the wall hanging, follow the usual procedure to outline your canvas and stitch the design from the chart. Block the completed needlepoint. Cut out a backing that is 1 inch wider on each side and 1 inch shorter on top and bottom than the finished needlepointed area. Place the backing fabric on the needlepoint with the right sides facing in. Sew a seam on each side of the backing and canvas, starting $1\frac{1}{2}$ inches down from the top and ending $1\frac{1}{2}$ inches up from the bottom of the stitched area. Make a few extra stitches at the top and bottom of the stitched area. Make a few extra stitches at the top and bottom of the seam to secure it. Turn the work right side out. Fold in the top and bottom edges of the backing fabric. Then fold down the top of the canvas and slip it into the backing so that it forms an open-sided hem. The hem should be a total of $2\frac{1}{2}$ inches long, with $1\frac{1}{2}$ inches of needlepoint and 1 inch of unworked canvas. The unworked canvas should be visible only on the back; the needlepoint

Wall hanging, stitched on ⁵⁄₁₀ penelope canvas with part of the canvas stitched at 5 mesh per inch and part with the mesh evenly separated at 10 mesh per inch, for a textural combination of needlepoint and quickpoint, in basket weave and continental stitches.

Drawing of the design for the Personification of the River Jordan. The background extends above the top of the figure so that the total size of the needlepoint area is 11 inches by 18 inches. In a complex design such as this, where the mesh is used in two sizes, it is helpful to transfer lightly the basic outlines of the design as well as the dimensional outlines for a guide as you follow the two charts.

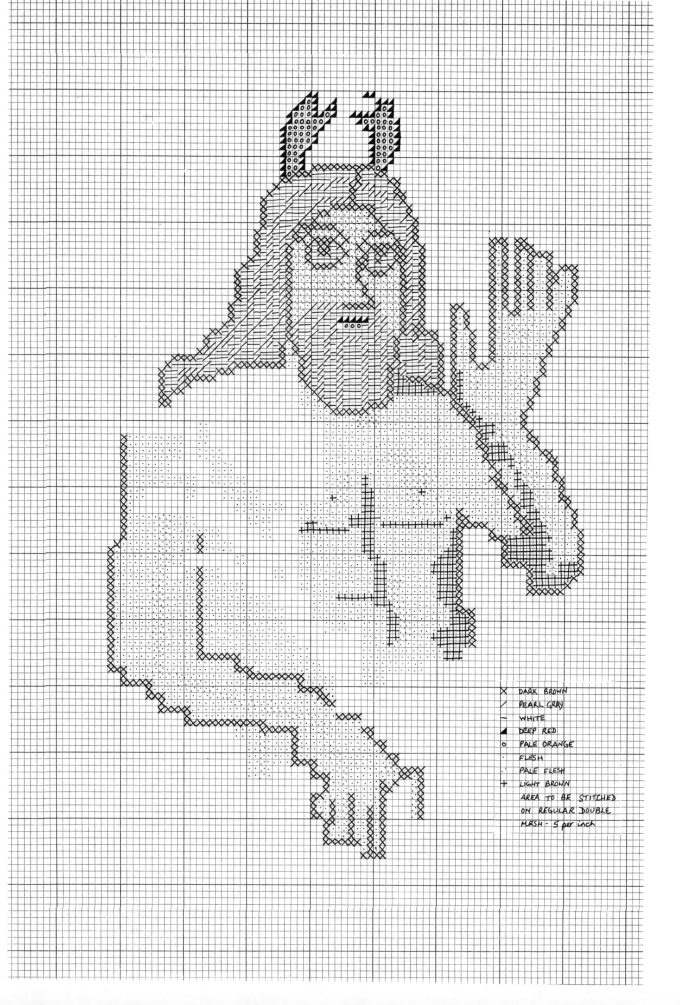

DARK BROWN
PEARL GRAY
WHITE
DEEP RED
PALE ORANGE
FLESH
PALE FLESH
LIGHT BROWN
AREA TO BE STITCHED
ON REGULAR DOUBLE
MESH - 5 per inch

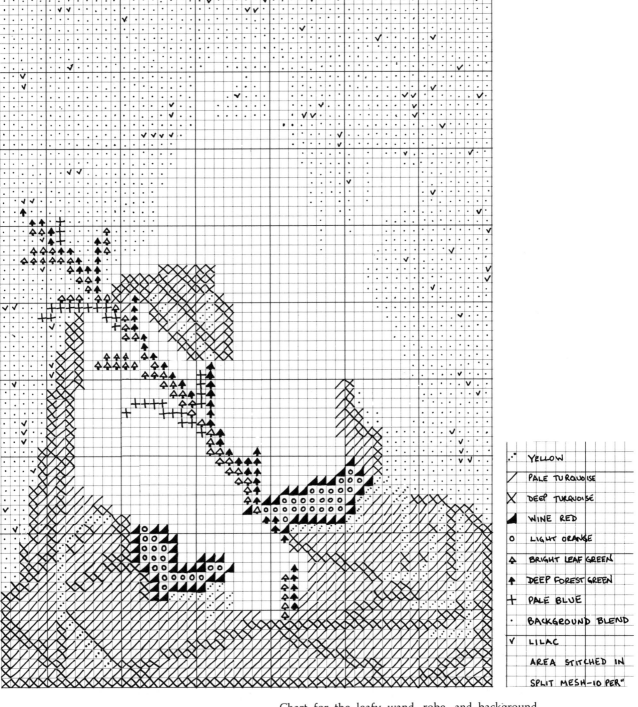

	YELLOW
/	PALE TURQUOISE
X	DEEP TURQUOISE
◢	WINE RED
o	LIGHT ORANGE
△	BRIGHT LEAF GREEN
▲	DEEP FOREST GREEN
+	PALE BLUE
·	BACKGROUND BLEND
V	LILAC
	AREA STITCHED IN
	SPLIT MESH-10 PER"

Chart for the leafy wand, robe, and background, stitched with four strands of tapestry yarn, in 5.5-yard skeins: wine red and light orange, 1 each, plus the extra yarn in the same shades from chart above; bright leaf green, 2; deep forest green, 2; pale blue, 1. In 40-yard skeins: background, a blend of light gold, deep gold, and gray is threaded in the needle with one strand each of light gold and deep gold and two of gray, requiring skeins: gray, 4; light gold, 2; deep gold, 2. Lilac accents, 1; pale turquoise, 2; deep turquoise, 2; yellow, 1. As you stitch the background, at the outlines of the figure smaller compensating stitches may be required to fill the canvas completely.

LEFT: Chart for the body, head, and hands, stitched at 10 mesh per inch in 5.5-yard tapestry yarn skeins: flesh, 8; pale flesh, 3; dark brown, 2; white, 1; pearl gray, 1; deep red, 1; pale orange, 1; light brown, 1.

comes up around the top and to the back so that only the stitched area is seen as you look at the front of the work. Sew the canvas and backing in place on a sewing machine set at 8 stitches per inch, using thread that is the same color as the background. Make the seam about $1\frac{1}{2}$ inches down from the folded top of the canvas and be sure that you sew through the backing at the same time so that the edge of the canvas is sewn to the backing as well as to the front of the canvas. Sew the bottom of the hanging in the same manner.

Slip in the rods that you have chosen so that their ends show equally at the sides of the top and bottom of the work. Where the top rod comes out of the hem on each side, tie one end of the cord you are using so that you can hang up the wall hanging. You can make the cord as long or as short as you wish, depending on the placement of the work on your wall.

Napkin Rings

Napkin rings brighten any table setting. The basic rings can be an inexpensive plastic set, an old set that you would like to cover, or rings cut out of cardboard paper towel rolls or metal orange juice cans. If you are cutting the rings, the metal cans have the advantage of being strong and stiff, but they can be dangerous to work with as they are very sharp when cut. If you use them, cover each edge as soon as you cut it with two layers of masking tape or adhesive tape. You can leave the tape in place and it will also protect your needlepoint when the rings are finished. Each ring should be 2 inches wide. You'll need a 12 mono canvas 12 inches by 16 inches, felt to line the rings, and Persian yarn in the colors and amounts given on the chart. This size canvas can be tricky, so try out

your yarn first, using two strands. If it doesn't cover well, use three strands of the Persian yarn.

Cut out four rings, or more if you want them. Draw outlines on the canvas for as many as you are going to make, following the dimensions in the diagram. The canvas size will accommodate four rings, placed horizontally, leaving 2 inches between each strip. If you are covering an existing set of rings, measure their circumference and width with a cloth tape measure and alter the pattern as needed to fit on a sheet of paper. Stitch the design—a fruitful border discovered in a Byzantine mosaic—the background, and the outline borders. Block as a group on the single piece of canvas.

Cut out each needlepoint strip, leaving about $\frac{3}{4}$ inch all around. Place face down on a work surface and put a ring on one of the strips. Bring one side around the ring and glue in place with white glue on the unworked canvas. Tape down if needed to hold the side in place while it dries. Do the same for the other rings. Fold in the extra canvas on the other side and glue it to the canvas of the first side so that the sides meet on the ring. Carefully stitch the two sides together using one strand of the background yarn. You need to make only a few stitches to secure the seam.

When the glue is dry, spread a thin coat of glue on the inside edges of the ring. Fold in the unworked canvas, smooth it in place, and allow to dry. While the rings are drying, cut out strips of felt the length and width of the stitched area. Try one out inside the ring. It should cover the inside and just meet where the two ends of the strip come together. Trim if needed. Cover one side of the felt strip with white glue and smooth it into the ring. For added strength you can sew around the top and bottom of each ring using a small overcast stitch and light, strong thread the color of the felt or the border.

Napkin ring, stitched on 12-mesh mono canvas with two strands of Persian yarn.

5 7/8"

2"

Drawing of the Byzantine border design with the dimensions of the needlepoint area for each ring. If you prefer, enlarge this pattern to life size and transfer the design directly to your canvas.

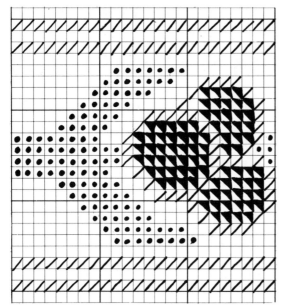

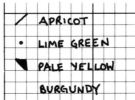

/	APRICOT
•	LIME GREEN
◢	PALE YELLOW
	BURGUNDY

Chart of one unit of the design, stitched in basket weave and continental stitches. You can change the background color to suit your decor, as the outline borders tie the colors of the design together. For four rings, using 5.5-yard skeins, you'll need: burgundy, 5; pale yellow, 3; lime green, 3; apricot, 3.

Doorstop

A colorful doorstop can be made using a standard terra-cotta-hued building brick. This design is derived from the undulating forms in the architectural Art Nouveau mosaics of Antonio Gaudi that were created in Barcelona during the early years of this century. It is worked on

Doorstop, on $8/16$ penelope canvas, stitched at 8 per inch with a full three strands of imported Persian wool. Some yarns will require four strands of Persian yarn to cover well, so check the yarn you're using before you begin to stitch the project. Stitch in basket weave and continental stitches.

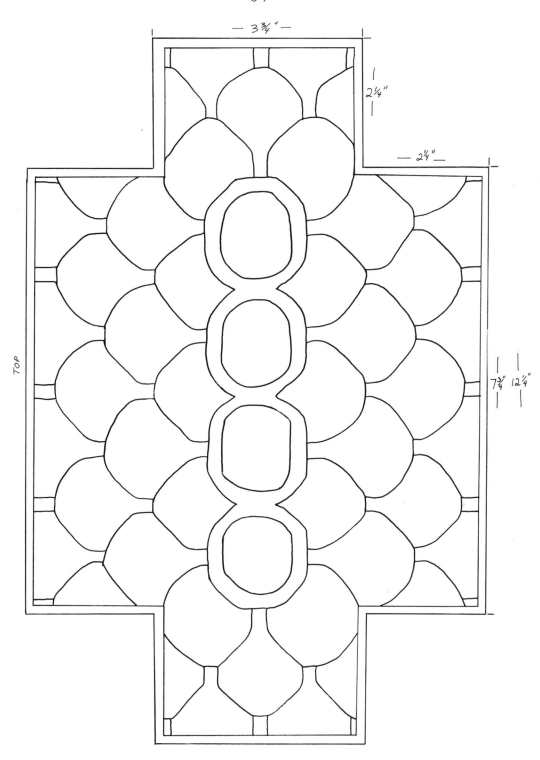

Drawing of the design, inspired by the mosaics of
Antonio Gaudi, with dimensional information. This
pattern can be enlarged and transferred to canvas.

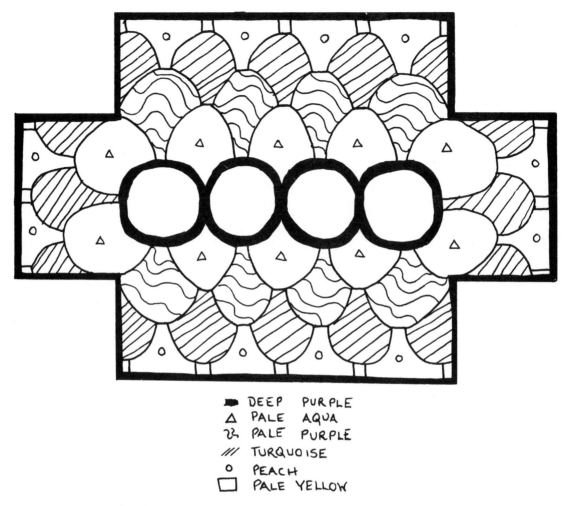

■ DEEP PURPLE
△ PALE AQUA
꙾ PALE PURPLE
/// TURQUOISE
○ PEACH
☐ PALE YELLOW

Color chart, for use if you transfer the design directly to your canvas.

an $^8/_{16}$ penelope canvas 15 inches by 11 inches. The yarn is a full-bodied imported Persian yarn, in 5.5-yard skeins, which covers the canvas well with the full three strands of yarn. You should try out a yarn beforehand, however, as this canvas sometimes requires four strands of Persian yarn to cover well. The amount of yarn given is for three strands, so if you need four of your yarn, increase the amounts of each color by one-quarter. For the bottom of the finished work you'll need a piece of felt 8 inches by 4 inches.

You can outline the design with the dimensions and pattern given directly on the canvas, or merely outline the basic shape and follow the chart without drawing the pattern onto your canvas to stitch the doorstop.

Block the completed needlepoint and trim the excess canvas so that there is a 1-inch border of unworked canvas around each edge of the stitched area. To assemble, place the needlepoint face up on a table. Thread a needle with strong thread. Start with any corner and lift two adjoining sides toward you. Fold the work so

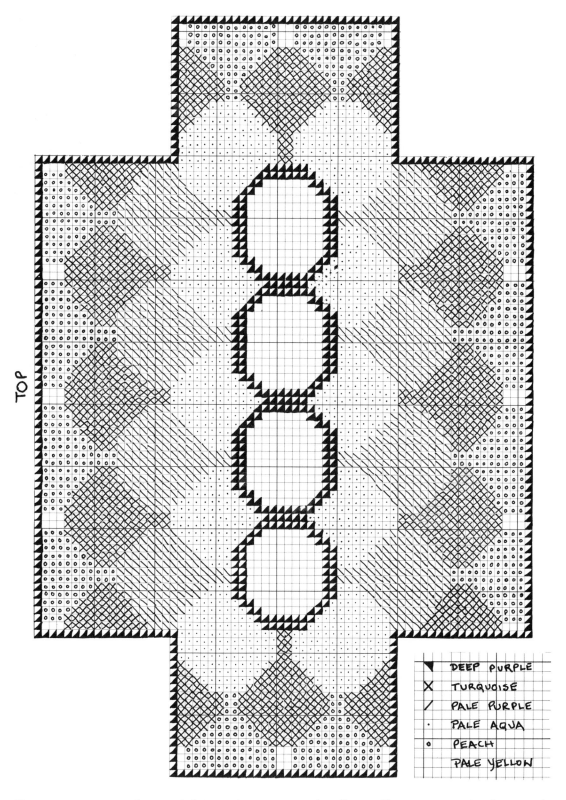

TOP

▼	DEEP PURPLE
X	TURQUOISE
/	PALE PURPLE
·	PALE AQUA
○	PEACH
	PALE YELLOW

Chart, yarns, in imported 5.5-yard skeins: pale aqua, 5; turquoise, 4; deep purple, 3; pale purple, 3; peach, 3; pale yellow, 1. If your yarn requires four strands, add one-quarter more yarn per color.

Pillow, on 14-mesh mono canvas, with two strands of Persian yarn, or one strand of soft tapestry yarn.

that the sides meet, forming one of the side seams of the doorstop. Sew the seam, starting from the inner corner where the sides branch out from the center of the stitchery, and sew up to the end of the needlepointed area. Having lifted the sides up and toward you, you'll be sewing from the wrong side of the work. As you complete each side seam, the needlepoint looks like an open box, with the right side of the design inside.

When all four side seams have been sewn, turn the needlepoint right side out and check the sides to make sure that no unworked canvas shows. If any is visible, add a few stitches with the yarn of the project. Place the needlepoint face down on a table and slip in the brick. Fold the unworked canvas down to the brick and sew in place at each corner.

Cut the felt to size so that the bottom of the brick doesn't scratch your floor. Sew the felt to the bottom edges of the canvas, using a small overcast stitch. If you prefer, you can glue the felt in place with a thin, even coat of white glue.

Pillow

Pillows are no doubt the classics of needlepoint. This is a patchwork potpourri, with twenty-nine motif areas comprising the total design. Each area was inspired by a different source, including ancient Mesopotamian columns, mosaic floors and walls in modern and traditional houses, along with original shapes, repeats, and motifs developed to complement the overall pattern. The canvas is a 14-mesh

	WHITE
/	TAN
◣	DARK BROWN
X	RUST
·	PALE BLUE
○	BRIGHT TEAL BLUE
+	OLIVE GREEN
—	GRAY
∷	APRICOT
⋈	ORANGE
■	DARK NAVY BLUE
⅄	ACID GREEN

Chart of the design, to be stitched in basket weave and continental stitches, in 40-yard skeins: dark navy blue, 1; dark brown, 1; white, 1; tan, 1; olive green, 1; pale blue, 1; rust, 1; bright teal blue, 1; gray, 1. Persian by the strand: apricot, 3; acid green, 3; orange, 2. (Enlarged version, pages 110–111.)

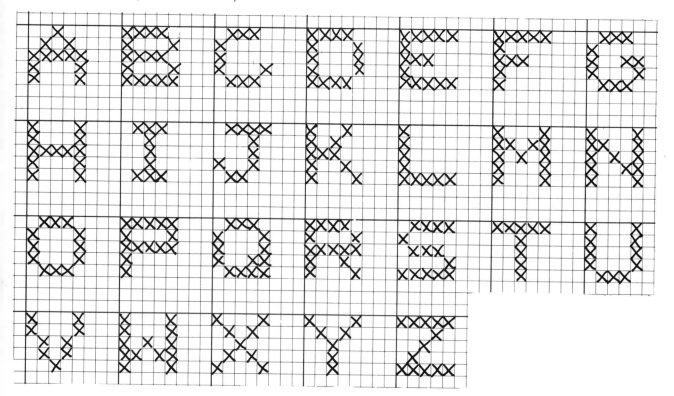

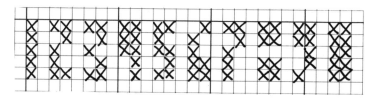

Chart of letters and numbers. To sign your work, choose your own initials and the numbers for the year, as shown in the square in the upper left-hand corner of the chart as three X's and '76.

mono, 12 inches by 11 inches, stitched in a combination of soft, lightweight tapestry yarn and Persian yarn in two strands in the colors and amounts indicated. You can substitute small amounts of yarn in colors that you have on hand, as a blend of yarns enhances the patchwork effect. Just be sure not to use the standard, slightly heavier tapestry yarn, as it is too bulky for the 14-mesh and will crowd your stitches. You'll also need $\frac{1}{2}$ yard of backing material—fine velvet in midnight blue is used here—1 yard of cording for the corded edges,

and loose pillow stuffing such as polyester fiberfill. When the pillow is stitched according to the chart, the finished dimensions of the needlepointed area are $8\frac{3}{4}$ inches by $7\frac{3}{4}$ inches, so you should mark an outline of this size on your canvas for a guide while stitching. If you prefer a larger pillow, use 10-mesh mono canvas 16 inches by 14 inches with standard tapestry yarn and three-strand Persian. Following the same chart, the needlepoint area will be 12 inches by $10\frac{1}{2}$ inches. A further variation, for a large floor pillow, is to use a $\frac{5}{10}$ penelope canvas, 27 inches by 24 inches, with quickpoint or rug yarn stitched five per inch, and you'll have a 24-inch by 21-inch needlepoint, following the same chart. Naturally, as you enlarge the size of the pillow itself, you must make corresponding adjustments in the size of the backing fabric and the amount of yarn.

Mark the outlines on your canvas and stitch the design according to the chart. Stitch your initials in the upper left-hand corner, following the chart for the right letters and numbers. If you prefer, you can repeat one of the design units instead of the initials and year.

Block the needlepoint and trim the edges of unworked canvas to about $5/8$ inch. Snip off the corners as well, so that they will form smooth points on the finished pillow.

Cut out a piece of backing fabric in the same dimensions as the trimmed canvas. To make the cording, cut 2-inch-wide strips of fabric. If you have enough fabric, cut the strips on the bias, or diagonal to the lengthwise and crosswise grain of the material. You'll need about 34 inches plus the allowance to sew each strip to the next. It's preferable to have as few seams as possible. When they are cut, sew the strips into one continuous strip. Place the strip on a table and put the cord on the wrong side of it. Fold the strip around the cord so that it is in the middle of the strip. Use the zipper foot on the sewing machine, as you want the seam to be as close to the cord as you can make it, and sew the cord in place inside the strip of fabric. Place the needlepoint face up on a table and place the cord around the edges of the stitched area so that the cord faces in toward the stitched area and the raw edges point toward the raw edges of the canvas. Pin it in place through the unworked canvas only, making sure that it is just inside the stitched outline border of the needlepoint. The cording should start at the middle of the bottom edge and run up and around the edges. When it reaches the starting point, curve the cord out toward the edge of the canvas so that it just overlaps the beginning end of the cord. When the cord is in place, sew it onto the can-

vas on the same line of stitching you used to sew the cord into the strip of fabric. Take out the pins.

Place the backing fabric on the needlepoint so that the right sides face in and pin it in place. Sew the backing to the pillow front around four corners and three full sides, leaving a 5-inch opening to stuff the pillow. Again, sew as close as you can get to the seams you have already made to hold the cording in place. Take out the pins and turn the pillow right side out.

Stuff the pillow, using shredded foam rubber or polyester filling, being sure to get the corners well stuffed. Then fold in the opening seam and sew it closed by hand, using the blindstitch and strong thread the same color as the backing.

Memo Pad

Memo pads are always useful, to jot down reminders, notes, and messages. A simple pad can be transformed with a needlepoint cover. Using the same principle you can also cover books of all sorts. The cheerful numbers, letters, and punctuation marks in this design are based on an idea employed in a mosaic mural at the Olivetti factory in Milan, Italy. The pad is $4\frac{1}{2}$ inches wide when closed, $4\frac{7}{8}$ inches tall, and has a thickness of $3/4$ inch. Mono canvas, 12-mesh, 13 inches by 8 inches, is stitched to the dimensions shown with two strands of Persian yarn, bought by the strand. To find the size canvas needed for your pad, measure its cover. Add the width of front and back plus the thickness, then the allowances for the fold and wrap-around edges of $1\frac{1}{2}$ inches, which will give you the width of the stitched area. Your canvas should have another 2 inches of unworked canvas around the needlepointed area as usual. Find the height by adding up the height of the cover, an allowance of 1 inch, and 2 inches of unworked canvas. You'll also need a piece of felt to line the inside of the pad cover and Persian yarn, worked with two strands in the needle, or three if you find that the canvas is

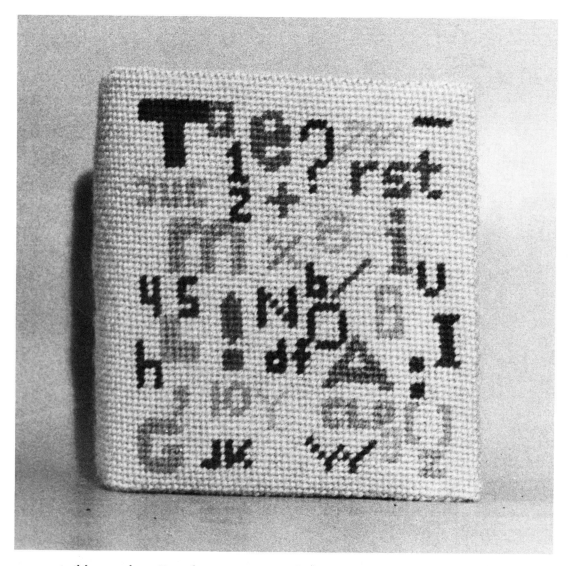

Memo pad, on 12-mesh mono canvas, stitched with two strands of Persian yarn.

not being covered well with two. This is another project that can be stitched with many of the small amounts of yarn that you have on hand; you can make the figures in as many colors as you like. To find out how much yarn you'll need to cover the background for your pad, work 1 square inch on the canvas you are using and multiply the amount of yarn it takes by the number of square inches in the canvas. You'll wind up with a bit more yarn than you need, as the figures do fill a fair amount of the canvas;

but, as said before, the extra yarn will always be useful.

Mark the outlines on your canvas and stitch the figures following the chart. With this sort of design you can repeat some or leave others out, depending on the space in which you are working. Block the stitched canvas. Remove the pad from its cover. Place the needlepoint face down and position the pad cover on the stitched area. Close the cover, wrapping the needlepoint around it to check the size. It should be wide

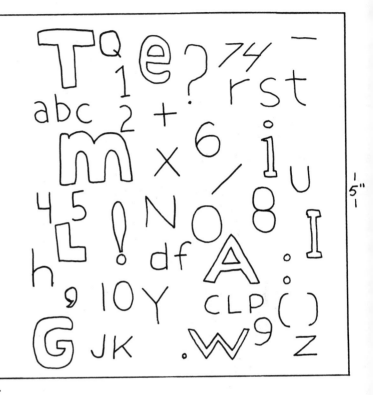

Drawing of the design, based on an idea found in a modern mosaic mural, shown with dimensions. You can transfer the entire design to canvas or use the chart.

and long enough to go around the edges of the pad without any extra canvas showing. If it isn't, add a few rows of stitches in the background color as needed. Then trim the canvas to ¾ inch. If it fits, trim right away. Spread a ¾-inch band of white glue around the inner edge of the cover and place it on the wrong side of the needle-

point. Form mitered corners by folding the corners of the canvas down first. Then fold down the top, sides, and bottom edges of the canvas. Let dry.

Cut a felt lining to fit inside the cover. Make sure that you cut the slit for the pad to slip into the cover. Place the lining in the pad cover and

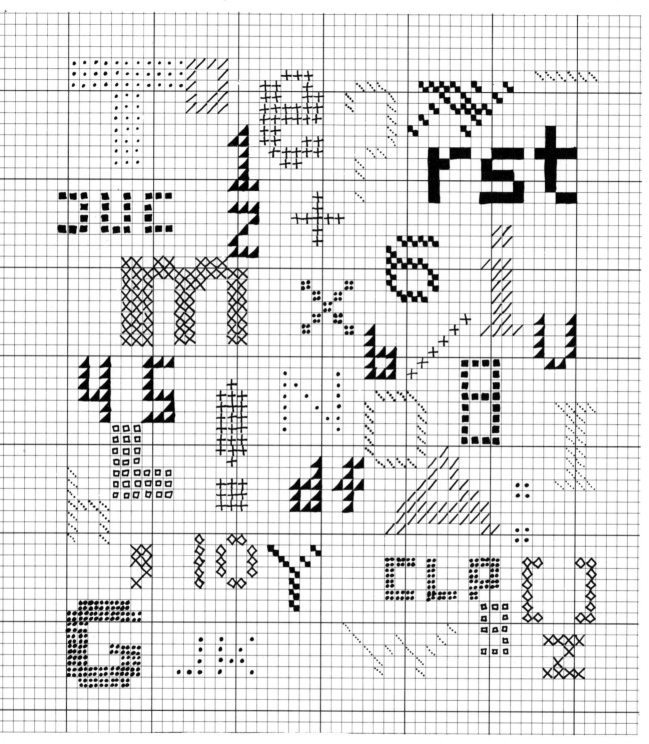

Chart of the design: letters and numbers in continental stitch, background in basket weave. Extend background stitching to cover needlepoint area for the back of the cover, as shown in the drawing. Yarn required: wheat background, 2 40-yard skeins; letters, 1 strand each.

	WHEAT
•	PURPLE
◢	BROWN
/	BLUE
■	GOLD
X	AQUA
□	DEEP GOLD
⋰	GREEN
::	LAVENDAR
†	RED
■	PLUM
◣	YELLOW
◇	ORANGE

fold the cover closed. If the lining extends past the side edges of the cover, trim it to fit. Then coat the wrong side of the felt lightly with glue and smooth it in place. Fold the pad cover closed carefully and let it dry in the closed position. Then slip the pad back into its slit and your memo pad is ready for use.

Watchband, on 13-mesh mono canvas stitched with two strands of Persian yarn.

Watchband

One of the beauties of needlepoint is that it can be combined so successfully with other craft media in the assemblage of useful articles. In this watchband the needlepoint canvas is sewn into a leather strap before stitching is begun; the strap is complete when you begin to stitch the needlepoint design and there is no need for blocking, as the structure of the band itself holds the canvas in shape. It is made out of fine, thin leather, worked around a strip of 12-mesh mono canvas.

The design is a variation of the classical Greek cresting wave pavement pattern, worked in two strands of Persian yarn. As there are 5 square inches of canvas, you'll need only small amounts of yarn in the colors shown. Before you stitch the charted design, try on the band to

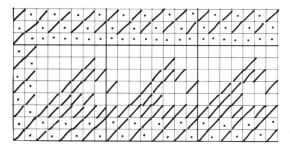

/	GRAY
	APRICOT
•	PALE BLUE

Chart of the pattern, based on a classical Greek cresting wave pavement pattern stitched in continental stitch and basket weave when possible. Yarn, by the strand: gray, 3; pale blue, 3; apricot, 3.

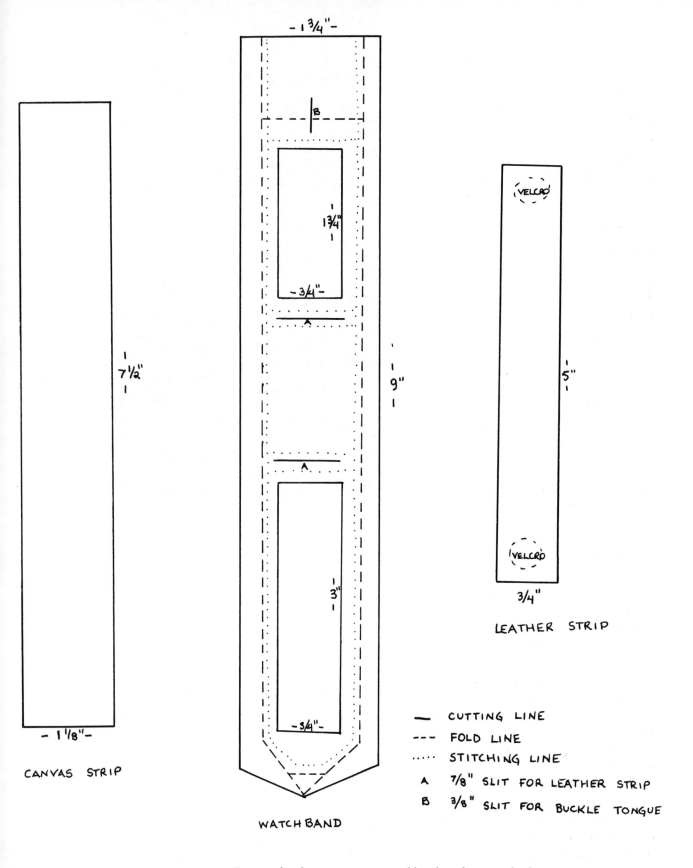

- 1 3/4" -

B

1 3/4"

- 3/4" -

A

9"

A

3"

- 3/4" -

A

WATCH BAND

7 1/2"

- 1 1/8" -

CANVAS STRIP

VELCRO

5"

VELCRO

3/4"

LEATHER STRIP

— CUTTING LINE

--- FOLD LINE

.... STITCHING LINE

A   7/8" SLIT FOR LEATHER STRIP

B   3/8" SLIT FOR BUCKLE TONGUE

Patterns for the canvas strip, watchband, and strip in leather.

discover where the buckle will close. Leave that opening in the mesh unstitched to allow the tongue of the buckle to pass through easily. For additional strength, if you have a hand-grip metal eyelet setter, it would be a good idea to push the mesh apart carefully at that point and slip in an eyelet. This will lessen the wear on the mesh. Then you can stitch the design and the watchband is ready for use.

To make the watchband, you'll need a 1¼-inch by 8-inch strip of 12-mesh mono canvas, a 4-inch by 12-inch piece of lightweight leather such as kidskin, a 1½-inch-wide buckle, a small round Velcro fastener, some rubber cement, and a leather needle for a sewing machine in the smallest size. An eyelet setter would also be useful if you have one, but it's not essential. As the leather is thin, you can cut it with a sharp pair of sewing scissors. Working from the wrong side of the leather, draw the outline for the leather band as shown in the diagram. Carefully cut out the two rectangular sections so that the mesh can be worked. Place the leather strip face down on a table and spread a thin coat of rubber cement on the back. Let it dry for a minute or two and place the mesh strip on the leather so that the canvas is 1 inch below the buckle end of the leather. Fold the thin side strips around the canvas. At the other end fold the leather to the canvas so that a point forms in the middle of that end. Put a dab of glue on the point and fold it to the back. Set your sewing machine at 8 stitches per inch, insert the leather needle, and sew the edges of the leather in place, starting at one side of the buckle end. Sew down along that side (working from the right side so that you can see what you're doing), around the tip, being sure to sew down the point, and then along the other side to the buckle end. Add four short lines of stitching across the center of the band for added strength, as indicated on the diagram. Cut a small opening in the middle of the buckle end and slide the tongue of the buckle into the slit. Put a bit of cement on the end of the leather and fold it back to the wrong side with the buckle in place.

Sew it in place, as close as you can get to the buckle. To hold the watch in place, cut a ¾-inch-wide by 5-inch-long strip of leather. Make two ¾-inch slits in the central portion of the band, being sure to cut carefully through the mesh as well as the leather, making the slits as far apart from each other as your watch is tall.

Stitch the needlepoint design. Then slip the leather strip into your watch, around the end bar from the top, under the watch and then up around the other end bar. Slide the ends of the leather strip through the slits in the band. Place the watch and strap face down. Fold down one side of the leather strip and cement half the Velcro fastener to the end. Cement the other half to the inside of the other end of the strip so that you can close the strip using the Velcro to hold it in place. If you have an eyelet setter, put in one eyelet before doing the stitching as described above.

Tennis Racquet Cover

Needlepoint an opulent cover for your tennis racquet or that of your favorite tennis enthusiast. This abstract design, which has a truly contemporary feeling, was developed from the basic shape of a unit found in a vaulted ceiling mosaic in Ravenna. It is stitched on 5/10 penelope canvas, 16 inches by 20 inches, with quickpoint wool yarn in the colors and amounts given. You'll also need an equal-size piece of heavy-duty backing fabric, such as sailcloth or canvas, and a strong, top-opening, 12-inch zipper. A sewing machine is helpful, but not essential, as you can stitch the seams by hand with fine results.

This cover fits standard wooden racquets. If your racquet is made of steel, it will probably require a slightly smaller cover. In this case, stitch the cover as shown, but try it out before you sew the seams. If necessary, you can make the seams ¼ to ½ inch deeper to fit while you are sewing it. This adjustment isn't always needed so it's best to make the cover in the

usual dimensions and fit it before making any changes.

Outline your canvas and stitch the design. Block as usual. Cut out the cover shape, leaving $\frac{3}{4}$ inch of unworked canvas around the needlepoint. Cut out a matching piece of backing fabric. Place the two parts together with the right sides facing in. Pin the edges through the excess canvas. Leave a 12-inch opening along the left side, which will be the right side when the cover is sewn and turned right side out. If your racquet is made of steel, slip it into the cover now to try out the size. Pinch each side together with your fingers where the seam will be—just inside the stitched area. If the cover seems quite loose, make your seam a bit farther into the stitched area. It shouldn't be too tight, so check carefully. Then sew the seams on a machine or by hand, using the backstitch. Make sure that you don't sew the zipper side closed. Take out the pins and turn the cover right side out.

Tennis racquet cover, on $\frac{5}{10}$ penelope canvas, in fine rug-weight or quickpoint wool in basket weave stitch.

Drawing of the design unit; detail from a ceiling in Ravenna.

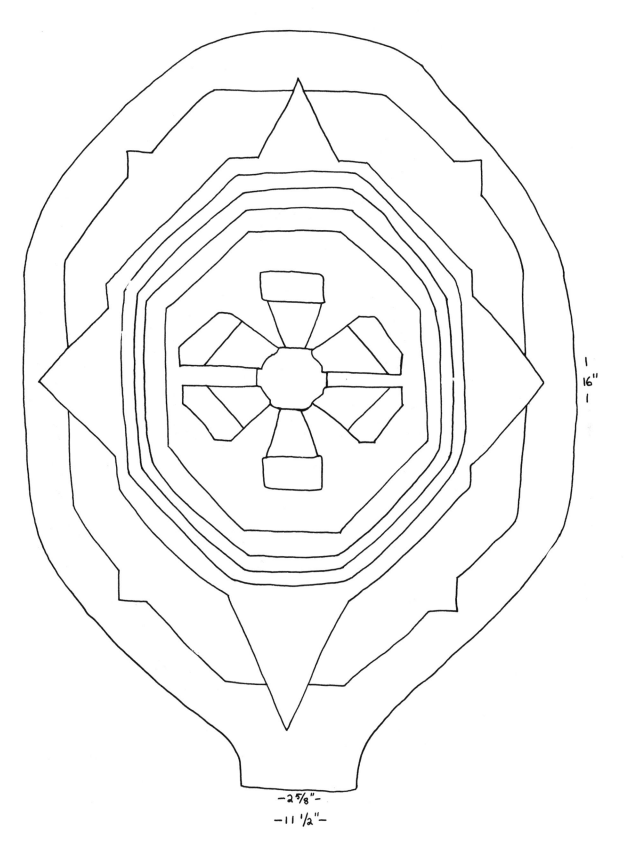

16"

−2 5/8"−

−11 1/2"−

Drawing of the design, as abstracted to fit the shape of the cover, with dimensions.

| | BRIGHT BLUE |
| WHITE |
| GOLD |
| PALE BLUE |

Chart, yarn needed, in 1-ounce packages: bright blue, 3; white, 3; gold, 3; pale blue, 2.

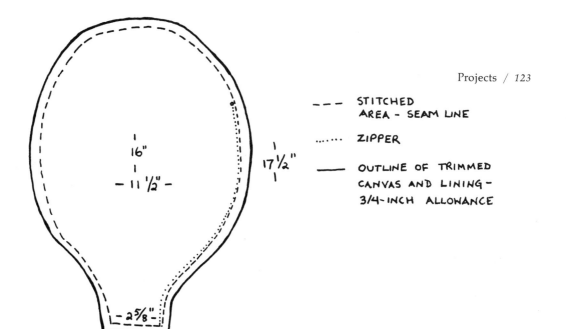

- - - STITCHED AREA - SEAM LINE

.... ZIPPER

——— OUTLINE OF TRIMMED CANVAS AND LINING - 3/4-INCH ALLOWANCE

Pattern for the cover, lining, zipper placement, and sewing lines.

The zipper opening is now on the right-hand side. Place the zipper in the opening, with the bottom of the zipper at the middle of the right side of the cover and the top of the zipper at the neck of the cover. When the zipper is closed its top should come to within two stitches of the end of the needlepointed area, and the tapes of the zipper should extend beyond it onto the unworked canvas. Open the zipper, pin it in place, and sew it onto the cover as directed on the zipper package. On the needlepoint side of the seam the stitches should be just inside the needlepointed area so that no blank canvas is visible. Take out the pins and turn the cover inside out. Fold in the neck edge of the cover and hem it in place, by hand or machine as you prefer. Turn right side out and your racquet cover is ready for use.

Mailbox

A good way to keep all your correspondence in one place is to stitch a mailbox. The one shown is made to cover a basic oval mailbox, which you can find in a variety store. You can

Mailbox, on $\frac{8}{16}$ penelope canvas, stitched in three strands of Persian yarn.

Drawing of the design, a variation of a Moroccan work.

also cover one on hand that needs a new look. The design is a version of a Moroccan work. It is stitched on an $\frac{8}{16}$-mesh penelope canvas 23 inches by 8 inches with four strands of Persian yarn in the colors and amounts given on the chart. You'll also need a slightly smaller felt strip to line the inside and a piece to cover the bottom.

If your mailbox has different dimensions, measure it with a tape measure to find the total outside width and the height. Then add 1 inch to the stitched area to compensate for the natural pull-in and the wrap-around edges. Before

you complete the final side edge of the needlepoint, wrap your stitchery around your box to check the size, as the width can be unpredictable. This mailbox is a standard size; you shouldn't have any difficulty finding one the same size and shape and can then use the same dimensions.

Mark the outlines on your canvas, stitch the pattern, and block the needlepoint. Cut out the felt to line the inside and the bottom of the box. Trim the needlepoint canvas to $\frac{3}{4}$ inch. Place it face down on a table and put the box on top of it to check the size. Then take off the box and

////   WINE RED
.....   DEEP YELLOW
ㄹㄹㄹ   PALE BLUE
☐   CREAM

Color chart of the drawn design.

5 1/4"

TOP

20 1/4"

fold the needlepoint in half, with the sides meeting and the right side of the stitchery facing in. Sew the sides together, with a seam just inside the line of stitches. Turn the needlepoint right side out, forming a tube.

Slip the box into the tube so that the seam runs along the middle of the back of the box. Put a thin coat of white glue just inside the top edge of the box and fold down the top unworked canvas and smooth it into place, making sure that the needlepoint covers the visible edge of the box as it goes around it to the inside. Turn the box over and spread a thin coat of glue around the bottom edge and smooth the canvas onto it, making V-shaped folds as needed so that it fits on the bottom evenly. Baste it in place through the folds to hold them in place. Then put a thin coat of glue on the felt and smooth it over the canvas. Let dry.

Try out the felt lining and trim, if needed, so that it just meets inside the box. When it fits well, spread a light coat of glue on it, slip it into the box, smooth it down, and allow it to dry completely.

Plant Stand

Plants are a part of many decorating plans today. One special plant can be shown to advantage on its own stand. The one shown is made out of wood, covered with a needlepoint design that is a variation of a Florentine inlaid marble work, dating from the early Renaissance. The canvas is a $4/8$ penelope, 27 inches by 10 inches, stitched in rug-weight wool yarn in the colors and amounts shown on the chart.

To assemble the stand, you'll need a hammer, wood glue, small nails or brads, and a vinyl floor tile or any other suitable covering for the top of the stand that doesn't mind an occasional

Dimensions of the needlepoint area to fit the mailbox shown. Check the measurements of yours and fit with a paper pattern before beginning your needlepoint.

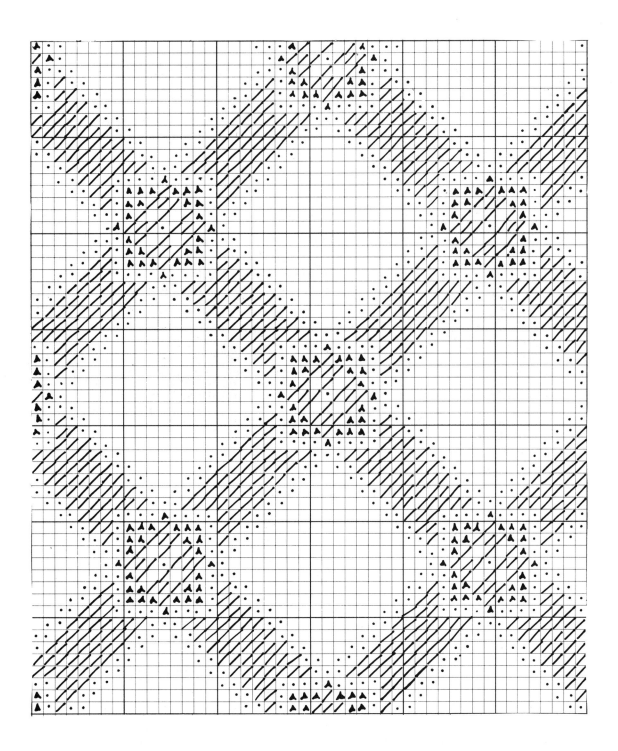

Chart of the repeating pattern for the mailbox. Persian yarn required by the strand: cream, 40; deep red, 26; golden yellow, 25; pale turquoise, 15.

╱	DEEP RED
▲	PALE TURQUOISE
•	GOLDEN YELLOW
	CREAM

Plant stand, on ⁴/₈ penelope, stitched in rug wool in the basket weave and continental stitches.

dousing with water. You can buy one tile and cut it to size with regular scissors. If you buy a tile, a pre-glued one will make your top even easier to put on. For the wood you can either order the pieces precut from a lumber yard or cut them yourself from a 6-inch-wide board. To make the stand exactly as shown, the wood should be $\frac{1}{2}$ inch thick and 22 inches long. You then cut four side pieces $5\frac{1}{2}$ inches long and the piece left will be 6 inches long to make the top. When using wood, always check its dimensions as the boards do vary in actual width and thickness from their specifications. You can easily compensate in the size of your needlepoint if

the size is different. To ensure that you will get a stand that works correctly, measure the wood. For the top of the stand the wood is cut to the same length as its width. For the sides measure the thickness of the wood and subtract it from the width. For example, in the stand shown, the wood is $\frac{1}{2}$ inch thick and 6 inches wide so the sides are cut $5\frac{1}{2}$ inches long.

To make the stand, take two of the side pieces. Put a thin coat of wood glue on one cut end and place it on the other piece so that the glued cut end is on the flat side right next to the end of the other piece. This forms a corner, as you can see in the diagram. Each corner is made

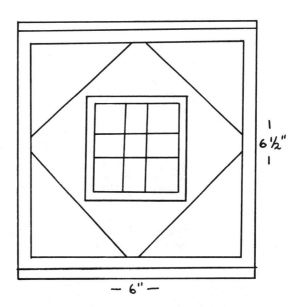

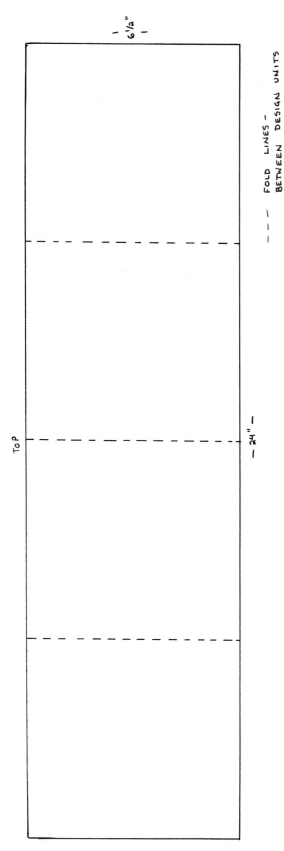

Drawing of the design, a derivation of an inlaid pattern dating from the early Renaissance in Florence, with dimensions of the unit, of which there are four in the entire stand.

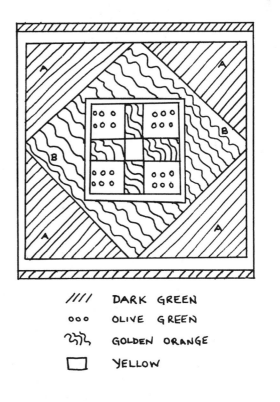

////	DARK GREEN
ooo	OLIVE GREEN
ｽﾞﾚ	GOLDEN ORANGE
▢	YELLOW

Diagram of the needlepoint area.

Color chart. Dark green (A) and golden orange (B) are reversed in every other design unit.

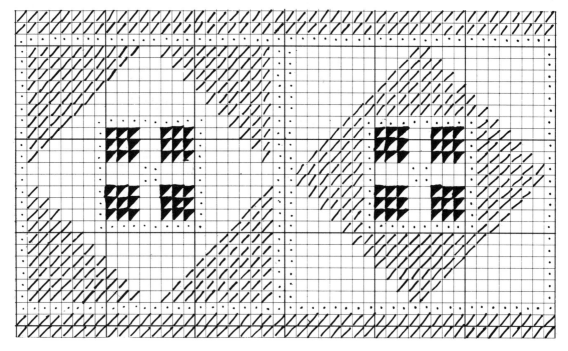

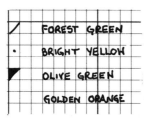

/	FOREST GREEN
•	BRIGHT YELLOW
◣	OLIVE GREEN
	GOLDEN ORANGE

Chart, to be repeated once, giving four squares in alternating sequence shown. Rug wool needed, in 1-ounce skeins: forest green, 3; golden orange, 3; bright yellow, 2; olive green, 1.

by placing a cut end on the flat side next to the cut end of the next piece. You will have formed a square out of the four pieces of wood with each corner overlapping the next piece of wood; this overlapping is done so that the top fits. Nail each corner in place with the brads. Place the top on the square of wood and glue it, then nail it to form the stand.

Check the dimensions of the stand and mark the outlines for stitching on your canvas. The diagram shown corresponds to the wood sizes as stated, so make any adjustments that you may need before starting the needlepoint. Block the completed canvas. Fold the needlepoint in half so that the sides meet and the needlepoint faces in. Sew a seam just inside the stitched area along the side. Turn right side out, forming a

tube. Slip the stand into the tube. Glue the extra canvas to the stand on top and into the inside of the stand on the bottom. Cut your tile or other top to size and glue or, if it is a self-stick tile, press it in place.

Blotter Ends

A basic blotter holder can be revitalized with new needlepoint ends. You can buy an inexpensive one in a variety store. The one shown holds a standard 11-inch by 14-inch blotter. The needlepoint requires a 14-inch by 14-inch piece of 8-mesh penelope canvas and four strands of Persian yarn in the colors and amounts given. You'll also need an extra blotter, sheet of

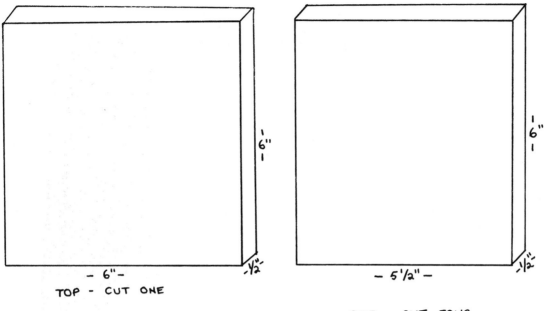

6"

6"

– 6" –

TOP - CUT ONE

– 5½" –

SIDE - CUT FOUR

SIDES ASSEMBLED - TOP VIEW

Diagram showing the parts and dimensions of the wooden stand and how it is assembled at the corners.

Blotter ends, on $^8\!/_{16}$ penelope canvas, stitched in four strands of Persian yarn.

oaktag, or piece of felt 11 inches by 14 inches to recover the bottom of the holder when you have put on the new ends.

The design is a Gothic pattern with additional borders. Outline the two strips of needlepoint on the canvas and stitch the pattern and borders. Block them in one piece and then trim to $^3\!/_4$ inch of unworked canvas around each edge. Remove the blotter from the holder and turn it face down. Remove the existing bottom liner, which is just glued down and usually peels off easily. Undo the inner edges of the ends at top and bottom so that you can put the needlepoint ends in place. Leave as much of the rest of the ends in place as you can, as only the insides need to be removed to cover them with needlepoint.

Fold the inside edge of the needlepoint around the inner edge of the blotter end and glue it in place. Do the other side the same way and let both sides dry. Place the holder face down and spread glue around the edge where you removed the inner edges of the ends. Fold the ends back around and into place, as they were originally. Tape in place while they dry. Remove the tape and spread glue around the edges of the holder back so that you can bring the rest of the canvas to the back of the holder and smooth it in place, mitering the corners. Then cover your new bottom liner with a thin coat of glue and smooth it in place on the back of the holder, covering the canvas edges and helping to secure them in place. Replace the blotter when the liner has dried.

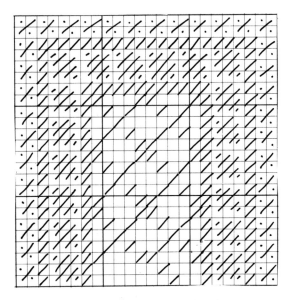

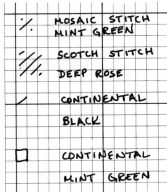

Chart of the design, with colors and stitches given, to be repeated to fill middle and bottom as shown so that the needlepoint area for each side is $3\frac{1}{8}$ inches by $11\frac{1}{4}$ inches. Yarns in 40-yard skeins: black, 1; mint green, 1; deep rose, 1.

Chart of the pattern in the central area.

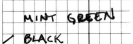

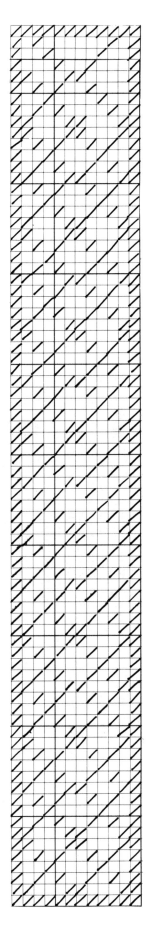

Clock Face

A clock face is an exciting way to add a note of originality to any room. You can buy a battery-operated clock movement for less than you might expect from a clock store. The hands come in many styles and are interchangeable, so you can buy the ones that you prefer. The frame is a standard 5-inch-square picture frame, with sides as deep as possible so that the works of the finished clock don't lean on the wall. You'll also need a 4¾-inch-square sheet of plywood with a hole drilled in the exact center to accom-modate the shaft which holds the hands of the clock, a small piece of wood to support the works, and some wood glue.

The canvas is a 12-mesh mono inches 9 by 9 inches, stitched in two strands of Persian yarn, bought by the strand in the amounts shown. The design was inspired by a pavement at Versailles. When you stitch the design, leave the center mesh unworked so that you can push the mesh apart and the shaft for the hands can fit through. When the needlepoint is blocked, place it face down on a table and center the sheet of wood over it, being sure to align the

Clock face, stitched on 12-mesh mono canvas with two strands of Persian yarn.

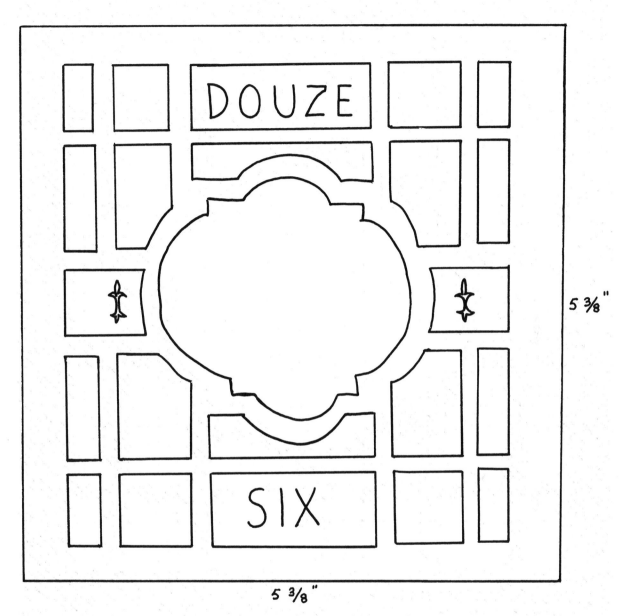

Drawing of the design, inspired by a mosaic pavement at Versailles, with dimensions, so that the design can be transferred to canvas or stitched by the chart.

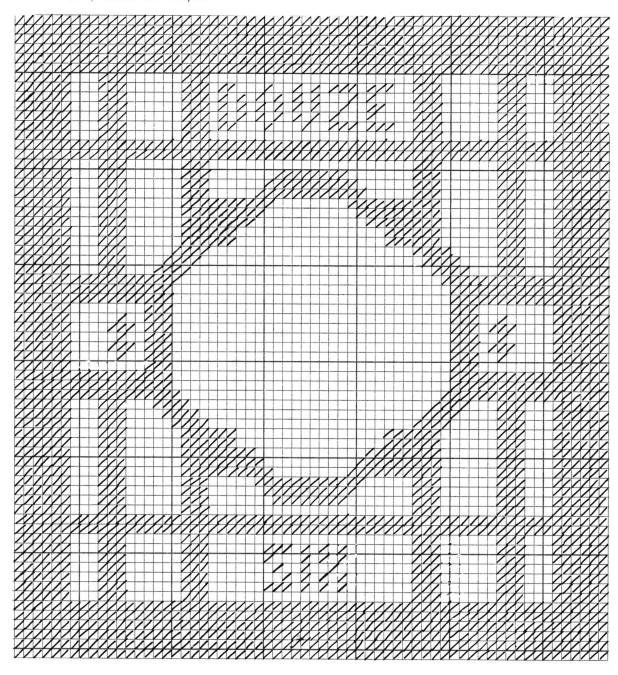

Chart. Yarns required by the strand: French blue, 20; white, 18.

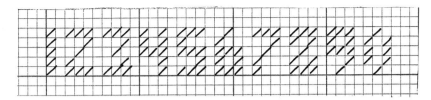

Chart of numbers, if you prefer to use them, omitting the French words for "twelve" and "six" and the fleur-de-lis. Substitute the numbers given, centering them well within the white sections.

drilled hole and the unworked center mesh opening. Spread glue around the edge of the wood and bring the canvas around it, mitering the corners. Baste the corners together to help hold them in place.

Try out the works, fitting the shaft through the hole and the unworked mesh. Mark the position of the bottom of the works and remove them. Glue the small piece of wood onto the back with wood glue so that it just meets the mark. Replace the works, put in the batteries, and fit the face into the frame.

Pictorial Reference Books

ANTHONY, EDGAR W. A History of Mosaics. Hacker Art Books, New York, 1968

ARGIRO, LARRY. Mosaic Art Today. International Textbook Co., Scranton, Pa., 1961

ARVOIS, EDMOND. Making Mosaics. Sterling Publishing Co., New York, 1971

ASHTON, DORE, et al. The Mosaics of Jeanne Reynal. George Wittenborn, New York, 1964

BERRY, JOHN. Making Mosaics. Watson-Guptill Pub., New York, 1966

BETTINI, SERGIO. Mosaici Antichi di San Marco a Venezia. Istituto Italiano D'Arti Grafiche, Bergamo, Italy, 1943

BLANCHET, ADRIEN. La Mosaique. Payot, Paris, France, 1928

BOVINI, GIUSEPPI. Ravenna Mosaics. New York Graphic Society, Greenwich, Conn., 1956

DALTON, O. M., East Christian Art. The Clarendon Press, Oxford, England, 1925

FISCHER, P. Mosaics: History and Technique. McGraw-Hill, New York, 1972

FURNIVAL, W. J. Leadless Decorative Tiles, Faience and Mosaics. W. J. Furnival, Staffordshire, England, 1904

GARY, DOROTHY, AND ROBERT PAYNE. Splendors of Byzantium. Viking Press, New York, 1967

GENTILI, GINO VINICIO. The Imperial Villa of Piazza Armerina. Istituto Poligrafico dello Stato, Rome, Italy, 1956

HASWELL, J. MELLENTIN. Mosaic. Van Nostrand Reinhold, New York, 1974

HENRICKSON, EDWIN. Mosaics: Hobby and Art. Hill & Wang, New York, 1957

HUCH, RICARDA. Early Christian Mosaics. Oxford University Press, New York, 1946

JUSTEMA, WILLIAM AND DORIS. Weaving and Needlecraft Color Course. Van Nostrand Reinhold, New York, 1971

KAHLER, HEINZ. Hagia Sophia. Praeger Publications, 1967

KAUFMANN, EDGAR. What Is Modern Design? The Museum of Modern Art, New York, 1950

KITZINGER, ERNEST. I Mosaici di Monreale. S. F. Flaccovio Editore, Palermo, Italy, 1960

LIBBY, WILLIAM C. Color and the Structural Sense. Prentice-Hall, Englewood Cliffs, N.J., 1974

LOWRIE, WALTER. Art in the Early Church. Pantheon Books, New York, 1947

MALCOLM, DOROTHEA. Design: Elements and Principles. Davis Publications, Worcester, Mass., 1972

MÂLE, EMILE. Religious Art. Pantheon Books, New York, 1949

MEYER, PETER. Byzantine Mosaics. Iris Books, Batsford, England, 1952

MILES, WALTER. Designs for Craftsmen. Doubleday & Co., Garden City, New York, 1962

MOREY, C. R. The Mosaics of Antioch. Longmans, Green & Co. New York, 1938

MURATORI, SANTI. I Mosaici Ravennati della Chiesa di San Vitale. Istituto Italiano D'Arti Grafiche, Bergamo, Italy, 1942

NEUMAYER, HEINRICH. Byzantine Mosaics. Crown Publishers, New York, 1964

PARKER, XENIA LEY. Designing for Crafts. Charles Scribner's Sons, New York, 1974

POWELL, HAROLD. Pottery and Mosaics. Charles T. Branford, Newton Centre, Mass., 1965

RICE, DAVID TALBOT. The Art of Byzantium. Harry N. Abrams, New York, 1959

ROSSI, FERNANDO. Mosaics: Paintings in Stone: History and Technique. Praeger Publications, New York, 1970

SCHAPIRO, MEYER, AND MICHAEL AVI-YONAH. Israel: Ancient Mosaics. New York Graphic Society, Greenwich, Conn., 1960

SEIDELMAN, JAMES, AND GRACE MINTONYE. Creating Mosaics. Macmillan Publishing Co., New York, 1967

SHERRILL, CHARLES H. Mosaics. The Bodley Head Ltd., London, 1933

STRIBLING, MARY LOU. Mosaic Techniques: New Aspects of Fragmented Design. Crown Publishers, New York, 1966

TIMMONS, VIRGINIA GAYHEART. Designing and Making Mosaics. Davis Publications, Worcester, Mass., 1971

TOESCA, PIETRO. I Mosaici—La Cappella Palatina di Palermo. Edizione D'Arte Sidera, Milan, Italy, 1955

UNGER, HANS. Practical Mosaics. Viking Press, New York, 1965

WHITTEMORE, THOMAS. The Mosaics of Hagia Sophia at Istanbul. Oxford University Press, London, 1943

WOLCHONOK, LOUIS. Design for Artists and Craftsmen. Dover Publications, New York, 1953

Index